A LITTLE SECRET ABOUT RELATIONSHIPS

NIKHIL KAPOOR

BlueRose ONE.com
Stories Matter
NewDelhi • London

BLUEROSE PUBLISHERS
India | U.K.

BlueRose ONE
Stories Matter
NewDelhi • London

For permissions requests or inquiries regarding this publication, please contact:

BLUEROSE PUBLISHERS
www.BlueRoseONE.com
info@bluerosepublishers.com
+91 8882 898 898
+4407342408967

ISBN: 978-93-5989-192-7

Cover Design: Sadhna Kumari
Typesetting: Pooja Sharma

First Edition: March 2024

Dedication

Dedicated to my best friend, Meeta, who is not just a legal partner (my wife) but the silent architect of my life. Her unwavering support granted me the space and time to navigate through myriad relationships - mental, emotional, and physical. Without her, these connections wouldn't have sculpted the canvas of our shared existence.

In Gratitude

I extend heartfelt thanks to each person who became a chapter in our journey. Their presence, however transient, contributed to the intricate mosaic of human connections. This book is a celebration of those who dared to be part of our lives, leaving an enduring impact on the tapestry of our shared existence.

Acknowledgments

Gratitude extends to every individual who played a part in my journey of relationships. Each encounter, be it brief or enduring, brought us closer and fostered personal growth. Meeta, my guiding force, illuminated the path, teaching me that love is boundless, a sentiment not confined by limits.

Reflections

This book is a reflection on the mosaic of relationships that enriched our lives. Each connection, whether fleeting or lasting, left indelible imprints on the canvas of our understanding of human sentiments. To label and constrain these connections is to undermine their essence, for genuine relationships defy categorization.

Learning from Love

Meeta's wisdom revealed that love is not a finite commodity; it's an expansive force that transcends boundaries. Every person who touched our lives became a teacher, imparting lessons on love, resilience, and the intricate dance of human connections.

The Unnamed Bonds

Real relationships defy definitions and flourish in the uncharted territories of the heart. To name or limit them is to negate their authenticity. In the tapestry of our experiences, these unnamed bonds stand as testament to the complex, beautiful, and often messy nature of relationships.

Preface's Essence

This preface lays bare the foundation of a narrative that transcends conventional notions of relationships. It is an exploration of the myriad connections that shape our lives, offering insights into the profound beauty and challenges embedded within the tapestry of human interactions.

~

The first time I met Love.

My heart was broken.

and I asked.

"How could you have betrayed me?"

And Love replied.

"It was your expectations. I am incapable of betrayal."

The second time I met Love.

My spirit felt crushed.

and I asked.

"How could you have hurt me?"

And Love replied.

"It was your reaction to the situation.

I am incapable of causing pain."

The third time I met Love.

My energy was drained.

and I asked.

"How could you have depleted me?"

And Love replied.

"It was your lack of self-love and failure to set appropriate boundaries.

I am incapable of depleting you."

The fourth time I met Love.

My entire being felt alone.

and I asked.

"How could you have abandoned me?"

And Love replied.

"I am always with you and can never leave you.

As I dwell within you."

The fifth time I met Love.

My soul felt vulnerable, naked and exposed.

and I asked.

"How could you have embarrassed me?"

And Love replied.

"It was your ego that caused you to feel embarrassed.

I am incapable of experiencing or causing shame."

The sixth time I met Love.

Anger rippled through me.

and I asked.

"How could you have taken from me?"

And Love replied.

"I cannot take from you.

I give while asking for nothing in return.

As I am unconditional."

The seventh time I met Love.

A deep sense of sadness pervaded me.

and I asked.

"How could you have fooled me and then used me?"

And Love replied rather gently and compassionately.

"Do not mistake someone's inability to love you.

For the truth of who I am."

And the eighth and final time I met Love.

I greeted it as an old friend.

Free from expectations, heartbreak, pain, shame and conditions

And Love embraced me and said.

"Now you truly know me."

Words by Tahlia Hunter

These are the lines which explains everything you wanted to know about relationship.

This book doesn't aim to offer self-help advice because I firmly believe that relationships are highly personal and unique experiences, and there's no one-size-fits-all solution. Instead, this book offers insights into various types of relationships, shedding light on their different aspects. Its goal is to encourage readers to refrain from imposing their own views and judgments on others' relationships without understanding the individual challenges and dynamics at play.

This book distinguishes itself from traditional self-help guides by acknowledging the inherent complexity and individuality of relationships. It recognizes that each person's journey in matters of the heart is unique, and what works for one may not work for another.

Instead of providing prescriptive advice or rigid formulas, the book adopts a different approach. It delves into a wide array of relationships, exploring their diverse facets, challenges, and triumphs. By doing so, it aims to cultivate empathy and understanding among its readers.

The central message is clear: We should resist the urge to judge or categorize relationships based on our own preconceptions and experiences. Instead, this book encourages us to appreciate the intricacies of each person's relational path. It serves as a reminder that behind each relationship lies a story, a set of circumstances, and a unique journey deserving of respect and consideration. In essence, it's a call to approach relationships with an open heart and a willingness to understand before passing judgment.

Contents

What is a Relationship?

A relationship is a profound connection, an intricate bond between two or more individuals, entities, or elements. It encompasses a spectrum of interactions, emotions, and dynamics that unfold uniquely in each context. Key features defining relationships include communication, shared experiences, mutual expectations, and often, a profound emotional attachment.

These connections manifest in diverse forms, from personal relationships such as friendships, family ties, and romantic partnerships, to professional collaborations like those between co-workers or business partners. The nature of a relationship is a complex interplay of factors, including trust, respect, mutual understanding, and the roles and responsibilities assumed by the involved parties.

Is a relationship an illusion?

Relationships are not illusions; they represent genuine connections and interactions between individuals or entities. However, the perception and experience of relationships can vary widely, depending on the people involved and their individual perspectives.

At times, individuals may harbor unrealistic expectations or idealized views of relationships, leading to disappointment or disillusionment when reality doesn't align with their expectations. This divergence from expectations can create a sense that the relationship was illusory. It is crucial, however, to distinguish between one's expectations and the actual existence of the relationship.

Unrealistic expectations or idealized views of relationships can stem from various sources and factors, including:

1. **Media Influence**: Movies, TV shows, and social media often portray romantic relationships in an idealized and dramatized manner, setting unrealistic standards for real-life relationships.

Societal norms and cultural expectations surrounding relationships may contribute to an idealized vision of what a relationship should be. External pressures to conform to certain standards can lead individuals to aspire to an unrealistic ideal rather than embracing the complexities of real connections.

Individual experiences, upbringing, and personal histories can shape expectations and perceptions of relationships. Past experiences, both positive and negative, can influence one's outlook and contribute to unrealistic expectations or a skewed understanding of what constitutes a healthy relationship.

Navigating these influences is essential for cultivating a realistic and fulfilling approach to relationships. Recognizing and addressing unrealistic expectations allows individuals to foster genuine connections based on mutual understanding, communication, and shared experiences, rather than being confined by illusory ideals perpetuated by external influences.

Raman and Devyani: Chasing Unrealistic Love Stories

In the vibrant tapestry of Mumbai, where dreams and reality often dance in tandem, Raman and Devyani were two souls intricately woven into the fabric of a city that thrived on passion and ambition. Their lives unfolded against the backdrop of a city that never slept, yet their dreams were influenced by the cinematic tales of love and romance that played out on screens and pages.

Raman, a meticulous software engineer with a penchant for precision, had grown up immersing himself in the fantasy worlds portrayed in romantic movies. To him, love was a symphony of grand gestures, passionate embraces, and a storyline that unfolded with the precision of a well-written code. Devyani, a dynamic marketing executive, had a similar narrative etched in her heart. Her vision of love included a partner who could decipher her unspoken emotions, orchestrate elaborate dates, and whisk her away on whimsical adventures.

Fate orchestrated their meeting at a friend's bustling soirée, and as their eyes met, it was as if the universe had penned them as the protagonists of their own romantic narrative. Sparks ignited, and the duo embarked on a journey of love, oblivious to the reality that awaited them.

However, their reel-life aspirations soon collided with the raw unpredictability of reality. The intricate dance of understanding and unspoken communication, portrayed effortlessly in movies, proved to be a challenge in their everyday lives. Raman's dreamy proposal fell short of Devyani's cinematic expectations, and her hope for intuitive understanding often clashed with the practicalities of human connection.

Their social media presence, carefully curated to showcase only the picturesque moments, inadvertently fueled the illusion of a flawless relationship. Admiring comments from friends and followers reinforced the image of the "perfect couple," concealing the struggles that lurked behind the filtered photographs.

As time unfolded, Raman and Devyani's relationship began to mirror the strains of their unrealistic expectations. The symphony of disagreements and discontent grew louder, leading them to contemplate the unthinkable – ending a story that had initially seemed destined for perfection.

In a pivotal moment, they engaged in a heart-to-heart conversation that unraveled the layers of illusion. It was in this vulnerable exchange that they acknowledged the toxicity of their pursuit for a love story mirroring the silver screen. With a shared realization, they decided to shed the weight of these unrealistic expectations, choosing instead to focus on the authenticity of their connection.

Their journey became a testament to the profound truth that real relationships transcend the confines of picture-perfect fairy tales. They began to appreciate the imperfections woven into the fabric of their love story — a narrative shaped by growth, compromise, and the genuine essence of two individuals navigating the chaos of everyday life.

This tale of Raman and Devyani is a reminder that love, in its truest form, is imperfectly perfect, a mosaic of real emotions and shared experiences, thriving in the midst of life's beautiful chaos.

2. Past Experiences: Positive past experiences or childhood influences can lead individuals to idealize certain aspects of relationships, making it difficult to accept imperfections.

Rajat and Sandhya: Breaking Free from the Shadows of the Past

In the tapestry of life, Rajat and Sandhya found themselves entangled in the intricate threads of their past, weaving a narrative of love and healing. Each carrying the weight of experiences that had etched deep imprints on their hearts, they embarked on a journey to untangle the knots that threatened to suffocate their budding relationship.

Rajat, scarred by the betrayal of a previous relationship, carried the heavy burden of mistrust. His ex-partner's infidelity had left him wounded, fostering an unrealistic expectation that every subsequent relationship must be shielded from the slightest hint of disloyalty. This expectation manifested as an intense jealousy and possessiveness in his newfound connection with Sandhya.

On the other side of the spectrum was Sandhya, whose childhood had been marred by the storms of her parents' tumultuous divorce. The echoes of constant arguments and discord lingered, shaping her longing for an idealized love free from conflicts. She harbored the unrealistic belief that true love meant an absence of disagreements.

Initially drawn to each other's warmth and kindness, Rajat and Sandhya's past experiences soon cast a looming shadow over their budding happiness. Rajat's insecurities fueled by fear of betrayal clashed with Sandhya's aversion to conflict. Their relationship became a battlefield of arguments, anxiety, and unmet expectations.

Recognizing the toll their past experiences were taking, Rajat and Sandhya chose a path of healing. They sought the guidance of a relationship counselor, a beacon of hope in navigating the complexities of their emotional landscape.

In therapy, the couple began unraveling the intricate threads that bound them to their unrealistic expectations. They discovered that no relationship is immune to conflict and that expecting perfection was a futile pursuit. Through guided introspection, they unearthed healthier ways to communicate, manage their emotions, and foster trust.

As the healing journey unfolded, Rajat worked diligently on overcoming his jealousy and trust issues. Simultaneously, Sandhya embraced the idea that healthy disagreements were a natural aspect of any relationship. They realized that their past experiences had shaped them but did not have to define their future.

Their relationship transformed into a canvas of growth and understanding. Rajat and Sandhya learned that true love was not about avoiding conflicts but navigating them with grace and empathy. The lessons from their past experiences became stepping stones, guiding them toward a relationship built on realistic expectations and genuine love.

United in their commitment to growth, Rajat and Sandhya's love story became a testament to the resilience of the human spirit and the transformative power of choosing to rewrite one's narrative. Through acceptance, compromise, and unwavering support, they emerged from the shadows of the past into the radiant light of a love that was as real as it was imperfect.

3. Peer Pressure: Social pressure from friends or peers who have high standards for relationships can lead to unrealistic expectations.

Navigating Romance Amidst Peer Pressure

Once upon a time in the charming town of Durgapur, there lived two young souls named Aryan and Anika. They were the best of friends, inseparable since childhood. Durgapur, with its quaint streets and warm community, was a witness to their beautiful bond.

As the two friends stepped into their teenage years, they found themselves surrounded by the enchanting whispers of love. Aryan's best friend, Kabir, and Anika's closest confidante, Riya, were already smitten with each other. Their love story seemed straight out of a Bollywood movie, with romantic gestures and sweet moments.

As the days passed, Aryan and Anika couldn't help but feel a subtle shift in their own friendship. The magic of Kabir and Riya's relationship cast a spell on them, and they began to see each other in a new light. Unbeknownst to them, the gentle breeze of love had started to swirl around, leaving behind a trail of blossoming emotions.

One day, as they strolled through the lively streets of Durgapur, Anika hesitantly spoke up, "Aryan, do you ever think about love and relationships?"

Aryan, trying to sound nonchalant, replied, "Oh, you know, it's not a big deal. Just something people do, I guess."

But the truth was, both Aryan and Anika secretly longed for a love as pure and magical as Kabir and Riya's. The peer pressure from their friends, who seemed to have set high standards for relationships, only fueled their desire for something special.

One evening, under the golden hues of the setting sun, Aryan mustered the courage to express his feelings to Anika. "Anika," he said with a nervous smile, "I think there's something more between us than just friendship. Do you feel it too?"

Anika, blushing and with a sparkle in her eyes, confessed, "Aryan, I've been feeling the same way. Maybe we should give this a chance."

And just like that, amidst the cozy atmosphere of Durgapur, Aryan and Anika's love story began. Their journey wasn't about grand gestures or extravagant moments; it was about the simplicity of two hearts realizing that they were meant for each other.

As their love blossomed, Aryan and Anika learned to navigate the twists and turns of romance in their own unique way. Durgapur, with its cobblestone streets and cozy cafes, became the backdrop to their love tale–a tale born not out of extravagance, but out of genuine emotions and the magic of friendship turning into something more.

And so, in the heart of Durgapur, where love stories unfolded like petals in the spring, Aryan and Anika's love story became a cherished chapter in the town's book of romance.

4: Lack of Relationship Education: Some people may not have had access to healthy relationship models or education about the complexities of relationships, leading to idealized notions.

Jai and Anushka: Navigating the Uncharted Waters of Love

In the vibrant heart of Bangalore, a love story unfolded between Jai and Anushka, two souls entwined in the delicate dance of romance. Their journey began in college, a whirlwind of emotions that carried them into a relationship, blissfully ignorant of the challenges that awaited them.

As their connection deepened, Jai and Anushka found themselves facing a common adversary – a lack of relationship education. Both had grown up in families where discussions about relationships were rare, and their understanding was predominantly shaped by the glamourous narratives of movies, TV shows, and the curated realms of social media.

This dearth of relationship education birthed unrealistic expectations. Jai and Anushka believed that love should perpetually echo the passionate intensity portrayed in movies. They thought conflicts were an ominous sign of a faltering relationship, and they should always exist on the ephemeral cloud nine of perpetual bliss.

As the months unfolded, the initial euphoria waned, and the unvarnished reality set in. Jai and Anushka encountered their first disagreement, a minor skirmish that left them both bewildered and hurt. Love, they believed, should be an impenetrable shield against conflicts, and the unexpected clash shook their foundations.

Feeling adrift in this sea of confusion, they sought solace from friends, only to find that their peers were similarly influenced by societal misconceptions about love and relationships. Well-meaning advice encouraged Jai and Anushka to pursue the elusive "perfect" partner, perpetuating the cycle of unattainable expectations.

Over time, misunderstandings and unmet expectations festered. Jai expected perpetual affection and understanding from Anushka, while she yearned for constant, spontaneous romantic gestures. When these expectations inevitably collided with the intricacies of reality, disappointment and frustration took root.

Realizing that their relationship was in peril, Jai and Anushka found themselves at a crossroads. They were equipped with love but lacked the tools to navigate the complexities of a healthy partnership. The vital lessons of effective communication, compromise, and the natural ebbs and flows of relationships had eluded them.

In a moment of clarity, Jai and Anushka decided to seek help. They enrolled in a relationship education program that served as a guiding light through uncharted waters. Here, they delved into the fundamentals of healthy partnerships – the stages of love, the art of communication, and the significance of setting realistic expectations.

As they absorbed this newfound wisdom, Jai and Anushka began to understand that love was not a constant, intense high but a nuanced journey with peaks and valleys. Conflicts were not indicators of failure but rather opportunities for growth. Real love, they discovered, demanded effort, compromise, and acceptance of each other's imperfections.

Slowly but surely, the landscape of Jai and Anushka's relationship began to transform. They learned the art of open communication, expressing their needs, and truly listening to each other. Setting achievable goals and embracing the imperfections that made their love unique became the cornerstone of their growth.

Their love thrived, not because it was perfect at all times, but because they had learned to navigate its intricacies. Jai and Anushka, once victims of unrealistic expectations, became champions for relationship education. They shared their story, emphasizing the importance of realistic expectations and effective communication in building lasting, fulfilling partnerships. Through their journey, they became beacons of hope for those navigating the uncharted waters of love.

5. Cultural and Societal Norms: Cultural or societal norms may promote certain relationship ideals that are not necessarily attainable or suitable for everyone.

Tale of Goa: William and Nisha

In the beautiful place called Goa, a happy and lively girl named Nisha from Banaras met a musician named William from Germany. They met at a café by the beach, and the sound of William's guitar made Nisha feel drawn to him.

They looked at each other, and a special connection happened. Even though they came from different places, Goa's nice atmosphere helped them fall in love. They enjoyed dancing and watching the sunset together.

But, deep down, there were some problems. Nisha grew up in a traditional Indian family, and they believed in getting married and having a family. Even though her family accepted her choices, they wanted her to find an Indian partner.

William, on the other hand, came from a free-thinking German family. They thought it was okay to live life freely without worrying too much about getting married. They valued doing what made them happy.

As time passed, these differences started causing trouble. Nisha felt stressed about introducing William to her family because she thought they might not like her foreign boyfriend. William was confused about why their love wasn't enough, and they argued a lot about getting married.

Their once happy love started to fade because of these problems. Nisha worried a lot about what her family would think, and William didn't want to commit to getting married, making Nisha unsure about their future.

One day, as they watched the sun set, Nisha told William about her fears and dreams. She wanted him to reassure her, but he honestly shared his doubts about settling down.

Even though they loved each other a lot, their different beliefs became too much. They sadly decided to go their separate ways, understanding that their cultural and family expectations were keeping them apart.

Nisha went back to her family in Banaras for comfort, and William continued playing his guitar in Goa. Their love story was special but also difficult, showing that sometimes love alone can't overcome the expectations of the world.

6. Fear of Loneliness: The fear of being alone or societal pressure to be in a relationship can make individuals settle for less-than-ideal situations or strive for unattainable perfection.

Navigating Expectations: Mitali and Abhinav

Mitali and Abhinav, both hailing from the charming city of Lucknow, met under the golden hues of a setting sun at a local cafe. Their connection was instant, fueled by shared dreams and a deep desire to escape the fear of loneliness that had haunted them for years.

As their relationship blossomed, so did their expectations. They believed that their love was a shield against the looming specter of loneliness, and with this belief came the burden of unrealistic hopes. They thought their love should fill every void, cure every insecurity, and erase the fear that had once gripped them.

In the beginning, their love seemed unbreakable. They spent countless hours together, their laughter echoing through the historic streets of Lucknow. Yet, beneath the surface, cracks began to appear. Mitali started expecting Abhinav to be her constant source of happiness, while Abhinav believed that Mitali could fill the emptiness in his life entirely.

Their unrealistic expectations led to disappointments. They started arguing over trivial matters, each disappointment magnifying their fear of loneliness. Loneliness was no longer just a fear; it was a reality they experienced within their relationship.

The beautiful, carefree days in Lucknow were overshadowed by the growing pressure to be everything for each other. The fear of being alone had transformed into the fear of being alone together.

One evening, as they strolled along the Gomti River, they finally addressed their fears and unrealistic expectations. Tears flowed as they confessed their loneliness and the toll it had taken on their relationship. They realized that expecting one person to be their sole source of happiness was an impossible burden.

With renewed understanding, Mitali and Abhinav decided to redefine their relationship. They embraced the idea that while they could be each other's pillars of support, they couldn't be the only ones. They rekindled their individual passions and reconnected with friends and family.

As time passed, their love evolved into a healthier, more realistic partnership. The fear of loneliness still lingered, but it no longer held them captive. They had learned that true companionship didn't mean erasing loneliness entirely but sharing it and growing together through life's ups and downs.

In the end, Mitali and Abhinav's story became a lesson in love and the importance of managing expectations. Their journey taught them that while love could be a balm for the fear of loneliness, it could not entirely banish it. Instead, they found that by facing their fears together and seeking fulfillment in various aspects of life, they could build a stronger, more resilient bond that would stand the test of time in the heart of Lucknow.

What if they mess it

If Mitali and Abhinav were unable to overcome their unrealistic expectations and the fear of loneliness continued to strain their relationship, their story might take a different turn.

As time passed and their expectations remained unmet, their relationship could become increasingly toxic and strained. Frequent arguments and disappointments might push them further apart, and their once-promising love might start to deteriorate.

The fear of loneliness could persist, causing them to cling to the relationship even if it was causing more harm than good. This fear might lead them to tolerate unhealthy behaviours or remain in a situation that made them deeply unhappy.

Ultimately, if they couldn't find a way to address their unrealistic expectations and fears, their relationship might eventually reach a breaking point. They might decide to part ways, hoping to find happiness and fulfilment separately. It would be a painful and difficult choice, but sometimes, it's necessary for individuals to prioritize their own well-being and personal growth.

However, it's important to remember that relationships can be incredibly complex, and the outcome can vary widely depending on the individuals involved and their willingness to work through challenges and seek help when needed. In some cases, even when things seem bleak, couples can find a way to heal and rebuild their connection.

7. Personal Insecurities: Insecurity about one's self-worth or fear of rejection can lead to seeking validation in relationships, setting unrealistic expectations for a partner to fulfil.

Shadows of Strength: Overcoming Insecurities

Raj and Simran had been inseparable since their childhood in the picturesque town of Shimla. Their love story was like something out of a Bollywood movie, and everyone in town admired their strong bond. However, as they grew older, personal insecurities started to creep into their relationship.

Raj had always been the popular one, charming and outgoing. Simran, on the other hand, was quieter and more introverted. As they both prepared to move to Mumbai for higher education and career opportunities, Simran couldn't help but feel insecure about how she would fit into the fast-paced, competitive city life.

In Mumbai, Raj quickly adapted to the social scene, making new friends and networking effortlessly. Simran, on the other hand, struggled to find her place. She compared herself to Raj and felt she was falling short in every way.

This personal insecurity led Simran to develop unrealistic expectations in their relationship. She began to demand more and more of Raj's time and attention, expecting him to fill the void she felt in her new life. Raj, in turn, felt overwhelmed by the pressure and began to withdraw.

Once loving and carefree relationship was now tainted by misunderstandings and constant arguments. Simran's insecurity caused her to become possessive and jealous, while Raj felt trapped and misunderstood.

It wasn't until they hit rock bottom that they realized something had to change. They decided to seek the help of a relationship counsellor in Mumbai. Through counselling, they both learned to communicate openly about their insecurities and fears. Simran admitted her struggle to adapt to the city's pace and her fear of losing Raj, while Raj confessed that he felt suffocated by the constant demands on his time.

The counsellor helped them set realistic expectations for their relationship and encouraged them to pursue their individual interests and friendships. Simran joined a local art class, where she met like-minded people, and Raj started giving Simran the space she needed to grow independently.

Over time, their relationship began to heal. They realized that personal growth and self-confidence were essential for a healthy partnership. Simran's self-esteem improved as she gained more independence, and Raj learned to appreciate the woman he fell in love within Shimla - a strong, caring, and talented individual.

Their journey wasn't easy, but their love for each other and their newfound ability to overcome personal insecurities ultimately strengthened their bond. Together, they built a life in Mumbai that was both fulfilling and harmonious, all while cherishing the beautiful memories of their hometown in Shimla.

8. Lack of Communication: Poor communication within a relationship can create misunderstandings and unmet expectations, fuelling idealized views.

Harmony Through Communication: Divya and Poornima's Journey

Once upon a time in a small town, there were two young women, Divya and Poornima. They were childhood friends who grew up together, sharing secrets, dreams, and countless memories. As they became adults, their bond deepened, and they decided to take their friendship to the next level by becoming romantic partners.

At first, everything was wonderful. They were deeply in love and enjoyed each other's company a lot. However, as time passed, they noticed differences in their expectations and desires within the relationship. The problem was that they weren't talking openly about it.

Divya, a free-spirited artist, wanted a relationship filled with spontaneity and adventure. She dreamed of traveling the world, experiencing new things, and cherishing every moment as if it were their last. Poornima, on the other hand, was practical and career-oriented. She saw their future together as stable and secure, with clear plans for finances and long-term goals.

Instead of discussing these differences openly, they made assumptions about each other's intentions. Divya thought Poornima was stifling her creativity, and Poornima felt that Divya was irresponsible and not taking their future seriously. Unspoken frustrations and misunderstandings began to mount.

One evening, as they sat in silence, Poornima finally gathered the courage to talk about it. "Divya," she began tentatively, "I feel like we're on different pages about our future. I want financial stability and long-term plans. But it seems like you want something entirely different."

Divya nodded, realizing it was time to share her desires. "Poornima, I love you deeply, but I've been feeling like I've lost my sense of adventure and creativity since we started focusing so much on planning and stability. I want a balance between our dreams and responsibilities."

With their feelings finally out in the open, Divya and Poornima began a journey of self-discovery and compromise. They learned to communicate openly and honestly, finding middle ground in their differing expectations. They decided to set aside a portion of their savings for adventures and artistic pursuits while still maintaining a responsible financial plan.

As they worked through their issues, their love for each other grew stronger. They realized that it wasn't the differences in their expectations that were the problem, but rather their inability to communicate and find common ground. Through understanding and compromise, Divya and Poornima's relationship blossomed into a harmonious blend of stability and spontaneity, proving that open communication is the foundation of any successful relationship.

9. Desire for Perfection: Some individuals may hold onto the belief that a perfect relationship exists, expecting nothing less. This mindset can lead to disappointment when confronted with real-life challenges.

Breaking the Chains of Perfection: Mitali's Journey to Balance and Support

Once upon a time in a quiet suburban town, there lived a girl named Mitali. She was a bright and ambitious young woman who aspired to excel in her studies. Her parents, Mr. and Mrs. Sharma, were well-intentioned but had always placed a high value on perfection. They believed that nothing less than perfection in every aspect of life was acceptable.

This desire for perfection extended not only to Mitali's academic pursuits but also to her personal life. They expected her to maintain impeccable relationships with her friends, classmates, and even herself. This constant pressure to be flawless had begun to take a toll on Mitali.

When Mitali decided to pursue her dreams of becoming a doctor, she enrolled in a coaching institute in Kota, a city known for its competitive exam preparation centres. The pressure to excel in these highly competitive exams was immense, and Mitali found herself struggling to keep up.

As days turned into weeks and then months, Mitali's stress grew exponentially. She felt like she was drowning under the weight of her parents' expectations. The constant fear of disappointing them was suffocating.

One evening, feeling overwhelmed and hopeless, Mitali contemplated ending her life. She felt there was no way out of this cycle of pressure and perfection. But just as she was about to take a drastic step, her phone rang.

It was Piyush, an old friend from her hometown who had also moved to Kota for coaching. Piyush had sensed that something was amiss with Mitali. He had seen her transformation from a lively, cheerful girl into a person consumed by stress and despair. Piyush decided it was time to intervene.

He rushed to Mitali's place and found her on the brink of despair. Piyush listened attentively as she poured out her feelings of inadequacy and hopelessness. Then, he convinced her to let him talk to her parents.

Piyush reached out to Mr. and Mrs. Sharma, who were initially unaware of the extent of their daughter's suffering. He explained how their desire for perfection had created unrealistic expectations and was pushing Mitali to her breaking point. He helped them realize that their love for their daughter should not be contingent upon her achieving perfection.

Slowly but surely, Piyush, Mr. and Mrs. Sharma, and Mitali began working together to break the cycle of unrealistic expectations. Mitali started receiving emotional support and encouragement from her parents instead of constant pressure. Her parents began to understand the importance of balance in her life.

Over time, Mitali's emotional well-being improved, and her academic performance followed suit. She realized that perfection wasn't necessary to be loved or successful. With Piyush's friendship and her parents' newfound understanding, Mitali found the strength to pursue her dreams without the crushing burden of perfection.

In the end, it was Piyush's intervention and the willingness of both Mitali and her parents to change that saved her from a tragic fate. They learned that love and support were far more important than any unrealistic expectations, and together, they forged a path towards a healthier and happier future.

10. Self-Help and Relationship Advice: Excessive exposure to self-help books, articles, or advice columns advocating unrealistic ideals can fuel unrealistic expectations.

Navigating Love's Reality

Once upon a time in the bustling city of Kanpur, there lived a young couple named Alka and Akash. They were deeply in love and had been together for several years. Their love story had always been simple and sweet, until one day, they stumbled upon a world of self-help books and relationship advice.

It all started innocently enough when Alka borrowed a self-help book from her colleague at work. The book promised the secrets to a perfect relationship and happily ever after. Curiosity got the best of her, and she devoured it in a matter of days. Excited by the newfound wisdom, she shared it with Akash, who was initially skeptical but eventually joined in the enthusiasm.

With their interest piqued, Alka and Akash began to explore the world of self-help literature. They read about communication techniques, love languages, and the importance of setting boundaries. They attended relationship seminars and followed online gurus who claimed to have all the answers. Their friends and family also chimed in with advice, sharing their own experiences and suggesting what the couple should do to strengthen their relationship.

As the months passed, Alka and Akash found themselves immersed in a sea of expectations. They started to compare their relationship to the idealized versions they had read about in books and seen on social media. Every disagreement or minor issue seemed like a significant problem that required immediate attention and resolution. They began to overanalyze every aspect of their relationship, from the way they communicated to the frequency of their romantic gestures.

Unrealistic expectations started to take a toll on their relationship. They felt pressure to be the perfect couple, always smiling, and always in sync with each other's needs. In reality, no relationship is without its challenges, but Alka and Akash had convinced themselves that anything less than perfection was a failure.

One day, after a heated argument about something trivial, Alka and Akash realized that they had lost sight of what had drawn them together in the first place - their love, acceptance of each other's flaws, and their ability to simply enjoy each other's company. They realized that the constant pursuit of an idealized relationship had caused them to drift apart rather than grow together.

Together, they decided to take a step back from the world of self-help books and relationship advice. They reconnected with the simplicity of their love and learned to appreciate the imperfections that made their relationship unique. They understood that there was no one-size-fits-all solution to love and that it was okay to have their own quirks and challenges.

Alka and Akash's relationship flourished once again, not because they followed a set of rules from a book, but because they rediscovered the authenticity of their love. They cherished each other for who they were, flaws and all, and realized that true love didn't need a manual - it just needed understanding, patience, and acceptance. And so, in the heart of Kanpur, they continued their journey together, stronger and wiser, with a love that was real and unburdened by unrealistic expectations.

It's important to recognize and address these factors to build healthier, more realistic expectations in relationships. Open communication, self-awareness, and a willingness to learn and adapt can help individuals develop more balanced perspectives on love and relationships.

Healthy relationships are built on communication, trust, mutual understanding, and shared experiences. They require effort, compromise, and emotional investment from all parties involved. While the dynamics of relationships can be complex and challenging, they are very much real and significant aspects of human life. The perception of an illusion in a relationship often stems from misaligned expectations or issues within the relationship itself rather than the relationship being inherently illusory.

Importance of Studying Relationships

Healthy relationships are built on communication, trust, mutual understanding, and shared experiences. They require effort, compromise, and emotional investment from all parties involved. While the dynamics of relationships can be complex and challenging, they are very much real and significant aspects of human life. The perception of an illusion in a relationship often stems from misaligned expectations or issues within the relationship itself rather than the relationship being inherently illusory.

Types of Relationships:

1. Personal Relationships:

These involve connections between friends, family members, and loved ones. They are often based on emotional bonds, trust, and shared experiences. Personal relationships provide a support system and a sense of belonging.

2. Professional Relationships:

Formed in a workplace or business context, professional relationships include connections between colleagues, supervisors, and clients. They are typically built on shared goals, cooperation, and professionalism, contributing to a productive work environment.

3. Romantic Relationships:

Involving couples emotionally and often intimately, romantic relationships are characterized by love, affection, and a commitment to a long-term partnership. These relationships play a significant role in personal growth and emotional well-being.

4. Social Relationships:

Encompassing acquaintances, casual friends, and individuals interacted with in social settings, social relationships may not be as deep as personal relationships but are crucial for socializing and networking. They contribute to a broader sense of community.

| Aspect | Personal Relationship | Professional Relationship | Romantic Relationship | Social Relationship |

|---|---|---|---|

| **Nature** | Informal, Intimate | Formal, Task-oriented | Intimate, Emotional | Casual, Varied |

| **Purpose** | Emotional support, companionship | Work collaboration, Career advancement | Love, companionship | Socializing, Networking |

| **Boundaries** | Often blurred, emotional closeness | Defined by job roles, hierarchies | Emotional and physical closeness | Social norms, context-dependent |

| **Communication** | Open, personal | Formal, Task-focused | Emotional, Expressive | Varied, Contextual |

| **Conflict Resolution** | Emphasis on understanding, compromise | Structured, Objective | Emotional communication, compromise | Adaptation, Flexibility |

| **Commitment** | Based on personal connection, mutual understanding | Contractual, Professional obligations | Emotional commitment, Mutual goals | Varies, Social context dependent |

| **Timeline** | Lifelong connections | Project or job duration | Varies, lifelong or temporary | Can be transient or enduring |

| **Expectations** | Often driven by emotional needs | Job performance, outcomes | Emotional fulfillment, shared experiences | Social interaction, mutual enjoyment |

| **Impact on Life** | Influences personal well-being, life choices | Affects career, professional growth | Shapes personal happiness, life direction | Adds social dimension, enhances quality of life |

| **Flexibility** | Flexible dynamics, evolves over time | Adheres to professional norms, structures | Evolves based on emotional dynamics | Flexible, adaptable to social contexts |

Note: Relationships are complex and dynamic, and these generalizations may not capture the nuances of every individual relationship within each category.

Key Elements of Relationships:

1. Communication:

Effective communication is essential for understanding each other's needs, emotions, and perspectives. It plays a crucial role in resolving conflicts and strengthening the connection between individuals.

2. Trust:

Trust serves as the foundation for many relationships. It involves the belief that the other party will act in one's best interest and be reliable. Building and maintaining trust is vital for the longevity of any relationship.

3. Mutual Respect:

Treating each other with respect is fundamental. This involves acknowledging individual differences, valuing each other's opinions, and respecting boundaries. Mutual respect fosters a healthy and harmonious relationship.

4. Shared Experiences:

Many relationships are built on shared memories and experiences. These shared moments contribute to a sense of belonging and connection, creating a bond that strengthens the relationship over time.

Understanding these types of relationships and the key elements that contribute to their success can guide individuals in building and maintaining healthy connections in various aspects of their lives. Whether personal, professional, romantic, or social, relationships enrich human experiences and contribute to overall well-being.

Conflict Resolution:

Conflicts are inevitable in any relationship. Healthy relationships involve the ability to address and resolve conflicts in a constructive manner.

Benefits of Relationships:

Relationships offer numerous advantages, including:

a. Emotional Support:

They provide a source of comfort, understanding, and companionship during both good and challenging times.

b. Personal Growth:

Relationships can promote personal development by exposing individuals to new perspectives, experiences, and challenges.

c. Social Integration:

They play a significant role in our social lives, helping us feel connected to our communities and the broader society.

d. Collaboration:

In professional and collaborative settings, relationships are vital for teamwork, knowledge sharing, and achieving common goals.

5. Maintenance and Nurturing:

Building and maintaining healthy relationships require effort from all parties involved. This may involve regular communication, empathy, compromise, and a willingness to work through difficulties.

6. Boundaries:

Setting and respecting boundaries is crucial in any relationship. It helps define the limits of acceptable behaviour and ensures that all parties feel safe and comfortable.

Let's Understand them thoroughly

1. Personal Growth:

Studying relationships allows individuals to gain self-awareness and insight into their own behaviours and emotions within relationships. This self-awareness can lead to personal growth by helping individuals recognize and address their strengths and weaknesses in relating to others. Through reflection and understanding, individuals can evolve, fostering a more well-rounded and emotionally intelligent version of themselves.

2. Communication:

Understanding how relationships work involves recognizing the importance of effective communication. Learning how to express thoughts, feelings, and needs clearly, and listening actively, is crucial for building and maintaining healthy relationships both personally and professionally. Effective communication is the cornerstone of meaningful connections, promoting understanding, trust, and cooperation among individuals.

3. Conflict Resolution:

Conflict is inevitable in any relationship. Studying relationships equips individuals with strategies for resolving conflicts in constructive ways, such as active listening, compromise, and problem-solving. These skills are vital for maintaining harmony and avoiding unnecessary strain in relationships. By learning effective conflict resolution, individuals can navigate differences without damaging the connection and, in fact, strengthen relationships through adversity.

4. Mental Health:

Healthy relationships are a cornerstone of mental well-being. Research has consistently shown that positive relationships with friends, family, and romantic partners can lead to reduced stress, increased happiness, and improved overall mental health. On the flip side, unhealthy relationships can contribute to mental health issues. Recognizing the impact of relationships on mental health emphasizes the importance of fostering positive and supportive connections.

5. Societal Impact:

Strong relationships form the foundation of strong communities and societies. When people have healthy relationships, they tend to be more engaged in their communities, support one another, and contribute positively to the overall well-being of society. Understanding the societal impact of relationships encourages individuals to value and invest in their connections, fostering a more supportive and harmonious collective environment.

6. Professional Success:

In the workplace, relationships are critical. Building rapport with colleagues, supervisors, and clients fosters a positive work environment and can lead to career advancement. Effective networking and collaboration depend on one's ability to form and maintain professional relationships. Recognizing the link between professional success and relationships encourages individuals to prioritize interpersonal skills in the workplace.

7. Research and Education:

The study of relationships is a core component of various academic disciplines, such as psychology, sociology, and family studies. Researchers explore different aspects of relationships, from their psychological underpinnings to their sociological implications. This research enhances our understanding of human behavior and informs educational programs and therapies aimed at improving relationships. By continually advancing our knowledge of relationships, we can develop more effective interventions and educational strategies.

Remember, relationships are at the heart of human experience and have profound implications for personal, professional, and societal well-being. By studying relationships, individuals can cultivate healthier interactions, better understand themselves and others, and contribute positively to their communities and broader society.

Types of Relationship in our lives

Family Relationships:

Family relationships are intricate connections between individuals related by blood, marriage, or adoption. They encompass various roles and dynamics, including parents, siblings, spouses, children, and extended family members. These relationships play a crucial role in shaping our identities and experiences throughout life.

Managing family relationships involves a range of skills and considerations:

1. Communication:

Effective communication is key to maintaining healthy family relationships. Open and honest dialogue helps resolve conflicts, express feelings, and build trust.

2. Boundaries:

Setting clear boundaries is important to maintain respect and balance within the family. This includes respecting each other's personal space, opinions, and autonomy.

3. Empathy:

Understanding and empathizing with family members' perspectives and emotions can lead to better understanding and closer relationships.

4. Conflict Resolution:

Conflicts are inevitable in any relationship. Learning to resolve conflicts constructively, through compromise and active listening, is essential for maintaining harmony.

5. Quality Time:

Spending quality time together fosters stronger bonds. Activities like family dinners, outings, or shared hobbies can create positive memories and connections.

6. Forgiveness:

Forgiving past mistakes and letting go of grudges can lead to healing and growth within the family.

Family relationships are dynamic and require continuous effort and understanding. By cultivating effective communication, respecting boundaries, practicing empathy, resolving conflicts constructively, spending quality time, and embracing forgiveness, families can build and maintain strong, supportive connections that contribute positively to each member's well-being.

Are family relationships authentic connections or merely obligations?

Family relationships can embody both authenticity and, at times, a sense of obligation or compulsion. While many family connections are nurtured by genuine love, care, and mutual support, there are instances where cultural, social, or familial expectations compel individuals to sustain relationships out of obligation. It's crucial to distinguish between the two and strive for authenticity in these relationships whenever possible.

Certainly, family relationships are incredibly diverse and can be influenced by numerous factors. Let's explore some real-life examples to illustrate the complexities and nuances:

1. Parent-Child Relationships:

- *Helicopter Parenting:* In some families, parents may excessively hover over their children, trying to control every aspect of their lives. While they often have good intentions, this can lead to strained relationships as children seek independence.

What is helicopter parenting?

Helicopter parenting is a style of parenting characterized by excessive involvement and overprotectiveness by parents in their children's lives. Parents who engage in helicopter parenting tend to closely monitor and control various aspects of their child's life, often to an extreme degree. This can include making decisions for the child, constantly hovering over them, and shielding them from any potential risks or challenges.

Helicopter parents typically have good intentions and want what's best for their children, but their excessive involvement can have negative consequences. It can hinder a child's development of independence, problem-solving skills, and resilience because they may not have the opportunity to make their own choices and learn from their mistakes. It can also lead to increased stress and anxiety for both the child and the parents.

The term "helicopter parenting" is derived from the image of a helicopter constantly hovering overhead, watching and directing the child's every move. It's important for parents to strike a balance between being involved and allowing their children to develop autonomy and decision-making skills.

Below is the story of Riaan and his parents to help you understand more about this.

Once upon a time in a quiet suburban neighbourhood, there lived a couple named Naman and Nisha. They were loving parents to their only child, Riyaan, who was a bright and curious young boy. However, Naman and Nisha had a tendency towards helicopter parenting, which would eventually have a profound effect on their lives.

From the moment Riyaan was born, Naman and Nisha were determined to provide him with the best of everything. They watched over him like hawks, making sure he was always safe and comfortable. As Riyaan grew older, this overprotective attitude intensified.

Naman and Nisha monitored Riyaan's every move. They chose his friends, his extracurricular activities, and even his hobbies. Riyaan's schedule was meticulously planned, leaving little room for spontaneity or self-discovery. While their intentions were to protect their son, they unwittingly stifled his independence.

As Riyaan entered school, Naman and Nisha became even more involved in his academics. They constantly checked his grades and pushed him to excel in every subject. They believed they were helping him succeed, but their constant pressure only added to Riyaan's stress and anxiety.

Years passed, and Riyaan grew into a young adult. He was an excellent student, but he lacked the self-confidence and decision-making skills that come with independence. He had never been allowed to make his own choices or face consequences on his own.

One day, Riyaan approached his parents with a plea. He wanted to go away to college, far from home, to experience life on his terms. Naman and Nisha were hesitant, worried about their son's safety and well-being. But they reluctantly agreed, realizing that they had sheltered him for too long.

As Riyaan ventured into the world on his own, he faced many challenges. But he also learned valuable life lessons. He made friends, made mistakes, and found his own path. Naman and Nisha, back at home, had to grapple with their newfound freedom and the realization that their overprotectiveness had hindered their son's personal growth.

Over time, Naman and Nisha began to reflect on their parenting approach. They understood that their intentions had been rooted in love, but they had smothered Riyaan's ability to be independent and resilient. They decided to change their ways, giving Riyaan the space he needed to make his own choices and learn from his experiences.

As the years went by, Riyaan blossomed into a confident and capable young man. He and his parents mended their relationship, understanding that the lessons of the past had shaped their present. Naman and Nisha realized that while helicopter parenting had initially affected their lives negatively, it was never too late to change and foster a healthier, more balanced family dynamic.

In the end, they all learned that parenting is a delicate balance between protection and allowing children to explore and grow independently, ensuring that love and trust are the guiding forces in a family's journey.

Supportive Parenting:

On the other hand, some parents provide unwavering support and encouragement, fostering strong emotional bonds. These relationships can evolve into friendships as children grow older. In supportive parenting, parents actively nurture their children's independence, allowing them to explore and develop their identities. This approach emphasizes open communication, trust, and a genuine interest in understanding and supporting the child's aspirations and challenges. As the parent-child relationship matures, it transforms into a partnership built on mutual respect and shared experiences. This supportive foundation lays the groundwork for children to navigate life's complexities with confidence and resilience.

So, what exactly is Supportive Parenting?

Supportive parenting refers to a parenting style characterized by nurturing, understanding, and empathetic behaviour toward children. It involves providing emotional support, encouragement, and guidance to help children develop their self-esteem, independence, and overall well-being. Supportive parents create a safe and open environment where children feel comfortable expressing themselves and seeking guidance when needed. This style of parenting often leads to positive outcomes for children's emotional, social, and cognitive development. Children raised in a supportive parenting environment tend to exhibit higher levels of self-confidence, resilience, and healthy interpersonal relationships.

Below is a story of 2 kids who had the unwavering support of their parents.

Once upon a time in a cozy neighbourhood, there lived a couple named Varun and Natasha. They were known for their unwavering commitment to supportive parenting. They had two children, Sonal and Anuj, who were the beneficiaries of their nurturing approach.

From the moment Sonal and Anuj were born, Varun and Natasha made it their mission to create a loving and supportive environment for their children. They believed in fostering independence while always being there as a safety net.

As Sonal and Anuj grew, Varun and Natasha encouraged them to pursue their interests. Sonal showed a keen interest in painting, while Anuj had a passion for soccer. Varun and Natasha enrolled them in classes to nurture their talents. They attended every art exhibition and soccer match, cheering on their kids regardless of the outcome.

The real magic of their supportive parenting was evident in their communication. Varun and Natasha always made time to listen to their children's concerns, fears, and dreams. They encouraged open conversations, making Sonal and Anuj feel safe discussing anything with their parents. This open dialogue built a deep sense of trust and understanding within the family.

When Sonal faced self-doubt about her artistic abilities, Varun and Natasha provided constructive feedback and reminded her that mistakes were part of the creative process. Anuj, too, experienced moments of self-doubt on the soccer field, but his parents reassured him that setbacks were opportunities to grow.

Through the years, Sonal and Anuj blossomed into confident and compassionate individuals. They credited their parents' supportive approach for their successes. Sonal's artwork was displayed in local galleries, and Anuj became the captain of his school's soccer team.

One day, as they gathered for a family dinner, Sonal shared her plans to study art abroad. Anuj expressed his desire to continue pursuing soccer at a higher level. Varun and Natasha, although saddened by the thought of their children leaving, wholeheartedly supported their choices. They knew that the values of independence, self-expression, and resilience they had instilled would guide Sonal and Anuj on their journeys.

Years passed, and Sonal and Anuj achieved their dreams. They often visited their parents, sharing stories of their adventures. Varun and Natasha's commitment to supportive parenting had indeed paid off. Their children had grown into happy, accomplished individuals who cherished the bonds of family, all thanks to the love and support they had received throughout their lives.

2. Siblings

Sibling Rivalry: It's common for siblings to compete for attention and resources, which can result in rivalry and jealousy. However, these dynamics can evolve into deep, lifelong friendships as adults. The experiences shared during childhood, the mutual understanding of family dynamics, and the bonds formed through various life stages contribute to a unique connection between siblings. As adults, many siblings find that the rivalry of the past transforms into a supportive and enduring friendship, grounded in shared history and familial love.

Below is a story on this context with multiple endings

Once upon a time in the small town of Meerut, there lived two brothers, Subham and Shivam. From the moment they were born, it was clear that they were as different as night and day.

Subham was the elder of the two, and he was known throughout the town for his charming personality and intelligence. He was an excellent student, always at the top of his class, and his teachers couldn't stop praising him. He had a passion for reading and would often be found lost in the world of books. Subham was calm and patient, making friends easily and rarely getting into trouble.

Shivam, on the other hand, was the complete opposite. He was the younger brother and had a wild spirit. Shivam was known for his mischievous pranks and fearless attitude. He was a talented athlete and spent most of his time outdoors, running, climbing, and exploring. Academics were never his strong suit, and he often found himself in trouble at school.

As the years went by, the differences between the two brothers became more pronounced. Subham excelled in his studies and decided to pursue a career in engineering. Shivam, on the other hand, struggled in school and decided to follow his passion for adventure by becoming a travel blogger.

Despite their differences, Subham and Shivam shared a unique bond. While they didn't always understand each other's choices, they respected and supported one another. Subham admired Shivam's adventurous spirit, and Shivam looked up to Subham's intelligence and discipline.

One day, Shivam planned an epic adventure - a trek to the Himalayas. While many doubted his ability to complete such a challenging journey, Subham stood by his side, encouraging him to pursue his dreams. Subham even decided to take a break from his engineering career to join Shivam on this incredible adventure.

The trek turned out to be a transformative experience for both brothers. Subham learned to embrace spontaneity and let go of his need for control, while Shivam discovered the importance of discipline and planning. They faced numerous challenges together, from unpredictable weather to treacherous terrains, but their bond only grew stronger.

Upon returning to Meerut, Subham and Shivam decided to combine their strengths. Subham used his engineering skills to create a blog platform for Shivam's travel stories. The blog became a massive success, showcasing Shivam's adventures and Subham's technological expertise.

In the end, Subham and Shivam proved that despite their differences, their unique qualities complemented each other. The rivalry of their early years transformed into a deep and supportive brotherhood. Together, they continued to explore the world, combining intelligence and adventure to create a life that celebrated both Subham's calculated precision and Shivam's fearless spontaneity.

Ending 1: Remaining Best Friends

Despite their differences, Subham and Shivam never lost the bond of brotherhood. As they grew older, they began to appreciate each other's strengths and started supporting one another. Subham helped Shivam with his writing skills, and Shivam encouraged Subham to break out of his shell and experience the world beyond books.

Over the years, they travelled together, experiencing new cultures and creating unforgettable memories. They realized that their differences were what made their adventures so exciting. Subham's knowledge and Shivam's adventurous spirit were a perfect combination. They became the best of friends and business partners, launching a successful travel and adventure company together. Their bond grew stronger with time, and they lived happily ever after, cherishing the unique qualities that once drove them apart.

Ending 2: Estranged Relationship

In Subham and Shivam's story, their differences seemed to create a growing divide between them as they grew older. Subham couldn't understand Shivam's reckless lifestyle, while Shivam felt judged by Subham's academic achievements. They started arguing frequently, and their conversations became tense and bitter.

One day, a heated argument escalated to the point where they decided to cut off all communication. They went their separate ways, each pursuing their own path in life without the other. Years passed, and they never reconciled. The once-close brothers became strangers to each other, their relationship severed beyond repair.

In this ending, Subham and Shivam's sibling rivalry eventually led to the complete estrangement of their relationship, a sad outcome for two brothers who once shared a home and a childhood in the quaint town of Meerut.

2. Siblings with Age Gaps:

Age gaps can create varying degrees of closeness in sibling relationships. Older siblings may naturally take on mentorship roles, offering guidance and support to their younger counterparts. Meanwhile, younger siblings can bring fresh perspectives, injecting energy and new ideas into the family dynamic. As everyone matures, these relationships evolve, with each member contributing their unique experiences and insights. The age gap, rather than being a barrier, becomes a source of diversity and richness in the tapestry of family connections.

3. Extended Family

Cultural Influence:

In some cultures, extended family plays a significant role in decision-making and support. Close-knit extended families can offer a strong sense of belonging, creating a network of emotional and practical support for individuals. However, this involvement may also bring about complex power dynamics within the family structure.

Decision-making may involve multiple voices, opinions, and considerations, reflecting a collective approach. While this can foster a sense of unity and shared responsibility, it may also lead to challenges in navigating differing perspectives and expectations. Balancing individual autonomy with the influence of the extended family can be a delicate task, requiring open communication and understanding.

Despite the potential complexities, the support and sense of community that extended families provide can be a source of strength and resilience, contributing to the overall well-being of their members.

Below is the story of Thakur Ranjeet Singh to help you understand more on this context.

Once upon a time in the heart of Jodhpur, Rajasthan, there lived Thakur Ranjeet Singh, a respected patriarch of his family and a shrewd businessman. Ranjeet Singh was known far and wide for his entrepreneurial prowess and his deep connection to the land of kings.

Ranjeet Singh had four younger brothers: Veerendra, Rajat, Harish, and Vikram. Each brother had his unique talents and strengths. Veerendra was a skilled horseman, Rajat a savvy trader, Harish a talented craftsman, and Vikram an astute accountant. Together, they formed a formidable team.

The Singh family had always been deeply rooted in their ancestral land, which they cultivated and turned into thriving farmlands and orchards. However, Ranjeet Singh saw the winds of change blowing, and he knew they had to diversify. So, with the support of his brothers, they ventured into various businesses – from textiles to trading spices.

As the businesses grew, so did the extended family. Nieces, nephews, cousins, and in-laws all found their place within the Singh dynasty. This close-knit network provided a strong sense of belonging and security to everyone. The family rallied around each other in times of joy and sorrow, ensuring no member was ever left in the lurch.

But amidst this sense of unity, power dynamics began to take root. Ranjeet Singh was the natural leader, given his age and experience. His decisions often carried the most weight, leading to some resentment among his younger brothers, who felt their contributions were undervalued.

This power struggle wasn't limited to the brothers alone; it trickled down to the next generation. The cousins, who had grown up together, found themselves competing for recognition and influence within the family empire. Family gatherings became less about celebration and more about subtle manoeuvres and positioning.

Despite the underlying tension, the Singh family's businesses continued to thrive. Their combined efforts and diverse skill sets allowed them to weather economic storms and emerge even stronger. Their strong bonds of kinship and shared history kept them together, even when disagreements threatened to tear them apart.

It was during a heated family meeting one evening, when tensions had reached their peak, that Ranjeet Singh proposed a radical idea. He suggested that they formally divide the businesses among the brothers, granting each autonomy over their respective ventures. This way, he hoped to alleviate the power struggles and allow each brother to shine in his own right.

Reluctantly, the brothers agreed to the plan. Over time, they nurtured their individual enterprises, and the Singh family continued to prosper. The cousins too, found their paths, collaborating and competing in a healthy and productive manner.

In the end, Ranjeet Singh's decision not only preserved their family's unity but also allowed each member to grow independently. The power dynamics that once threatened to consume them were channeled into healthy competition, propelling the Singh family and their businesses to new heights, while the bonds of kinship remained as strong as ever. The legacy of Thakur Ranjeet Singh and his brothers continued to flourish, reminding them all that, in the end, it was family that mattered most.

Geographical Distance:

When family members live far apart, maintaining relationships can be challenging. Technology has made it easier to stay connected, but it can't replace face-to-face interactions.

Below is the story about the same context

Minal and Naman, born and raised in the picturesque town of Jabalpur, had always cherished the simplicity of their hometown. The quiet streets, familiar faces, and rich culture were ingrained in their hearts. Yet, they were well aware of the opportunities that awaited their children, Nitya and Nimish, in far-off lands.

As Nitya pursued her dreams in Canada, studying engineering at a prestigious university, Nimish ventured to New Zealand to explore his passion for environmental science. Although the geographical distance seemed vast, the bond within their family remained unbreakable, thanks to modern technology. Video calls and instant messaging brought them together, bridging the miles that separated them.

Minal and Naman had a profound understanding of their children's ambitions and aspirations. They didn't want their kids to be tethered to their hometown, even if it meant staying apart. The parents were proud of Nitya and Nimish's accomplishments and supported them wholeheartedly. They believed in the importance of growth and the pursuit of one's dreams, just as they had once dreamed for themselves.

The kids, in return, were deeply respectful of their parents' wishes. They knew that Minal and Naman had sacrificed much to provide them with a good education and ample opportunities. They promised to stay closely connected, sharing their lives through screens and occasionally making the long journey back home.

Over the years, Nitya and Nimish excelled in their respective fields. Nitya became an accomplished engineer working on cutting-edge technology, and Nimish became an environmentalist making strides in sustainability. Despite the physical distance, the siblings continued to be each other's pillars of support, often brainstorming and sharing ideas across continents.

As time passed, Minal and Naman gracefully embraced the quietude of their hometown. They took solace in the knowledge that their children were flourishing. Their bond with Nitya and Nimish grew stronger through virtual connections, and they eagerly awaited their visits.

The grandchildren arrived eventually, bringing an extra layer of warmth and joy to the family. The kids, too, became adept at navigating technology to keep in touch with their grandparents. They would chat, share school stories, and celebrate birthdays together, albeit through screens.

Minal and Naman, despite their initial reservations about leaving Jabalpur, found solace in the knowledge that their decision had allowed their children to soar. The geographical distance never severed their familial ties, thanks to the wonders of modern technology. In this tale of love, support, and the pursuit of dreams, the family proved that no matter the physical separation, their hearts remained eternally connected.

4. Marital Relationships

Arranged Marriages:

Arranged marriages are common in various cultures. They often involve couples with limited initial familiarity. Despite this, these relationships can evolve into deep love and companionship over time.

Pros:

1. Family Support:

Arranged marriages benefit from strong family support, offering couples guidance and assistance in navigating challenges, thereby building a robust support system.

2. Compatibility:

Factors like religion, culture, and social status, carefully considered by families, contribute to better compatibility between the couple, fostering a foundation for a lasting relationship.

3. Reduced Pressure for Dating:

The absence of the pressure to find a partner independently can be advantageous, especially for individuals who may struggle with dating or experience social anxiety.

4. Lower Divorce Rates:

Some studies indicate that arranged marriages may have lower divorce rates, attributed to the emphasis on compatibility and the commitment established within the marriage.

Cons:

1. Lack of Personal Choice:

Arranged marriages may limit individual choice, leading to feelings of being compelled into a relationship that one might not have chosen independently.

2. Pressure to Conform:

Couples may experience pressure to conform to family expectations, potentially leading to unhappiness if their genuine connection is compromised.

3. Compatibility Issues:

Despite efforts towards compatibility, it is not always guaranteed, and couples may discover significant differences only after marriage, posing potential challenges.

4. Limited Romance:

The romantic aspect of love may not develop organically in arranged marriages, requiring couples to actively work on building that connection over time.

It is crucial to recognize that experiences in arranged marriages can vary widely depending on cultural and individual factors. While some couples find great happiness and fulfilment in arranged marriages, others may encounter significant challenges.

Divorce and Blended Families:

Family dynamics can become even more intricate when divorce and remarriage occur. New stepfamily dynamics can be challenging to navigate.

Below is a case-study related in same context.

Title: Exploring the Transformative Effects of Divorce and Remarriage on Family Dynamics: A Case Study of Two Couples - Sudha & Vikram and Jay & Jayantika

Abstract:

This study delves into the intricate and multifaceted consequences of divorce and remarriage on family dynamics, presenting an in-depth analysis of two couples: Sudha & Vikram and Jay & Jayantika. These significant life events can reshape the structure and functioning of families, impacting emotional, psychological, and social aspects. Through comprehensive examination, we aim to unravel the complexities of these repercussions on both nuclear and extended family units.

Introduction:

With divorce and remarriage becoming increasingly prevalent in contemporary society, understanding the implications for family dynamics is paramount. Sudha & Vikram and Jay & Jayantika serve as poignant case studies, offering insights into the evolving relationships between spouses, children, and extended family members during these transitions.

Methodology:

This study employed in-depth interviews with Sudha, Vikram, Jay, Jayantika, and selected family members. These interviews were complemented by surveys and observations to gather extensive data on their family dynamics.

Findings:

1. Emotional Impact:

a. Sudha & Vikram:

- Initial emotional distress followed Sudha and Vikram's divorce, affecting both parents and children.

- Over time, the emotional healing allowed for the establishment of a cordial co-parenting relationship.

b. Jay & Jayantika:

- Emotional challenges ensued after Jay and Jayantika's divorce, particularly impacting their children.

- Both parents grappled with finding new partners, contributing to emotional instability within the family.

2. Parent-Child Relationships:

a. Sudha & Vikram:

- Children faced adaptation challenges to living in two households, causing initial confusion and stress.

- Open communication and consistent parenting strategies contributed to stabilizing parent-child relationships.

b. Jay & Jayantika:

- The children encountered difficulties adjusting to their parents' new partners.

- Counselling played a pivotal role in addressing emotional strains on parent-child relationships.

3. Remarriage:

a. Sudha & Vikram:

- Vikram's remarriage introduced a new dynamic, necessitating Sudha's adjustment to her children's stepmother.

- The extended family's mixed reactions to Vikram's remarriage influenced their interactions.

b. Jay & Jayantika:

- Jay's remarriage significantly impacted the family, leading to changes in financial responsibilities and custody arrangements.

- Jayantika's feelings of jealousy and insecurity influenced her relationship with Jay and their children.

4. Extended Family:

a. Sudha & Vikram:

- Sudha's parents offered emotional support during the divorce but had mixed feelings about Vikram's remarriage.

b. Jay & Jayantika:

- Jay's extended family was more supportive of his remarriage, while Jayantika's family expressed concerns about the children's well-being.

Conclusion:

This study underscores the profound and enduring effects of divorce and remarriage on family dynamics. Emotional challenges, adjustments in parent-child relationships, and the introduction of new family members all contribute significantly to reshaping these dynamics. The extended family's reactions can further influence the overall family structure. Understanding these impacts is crucial for individuals and professionals involved in counselling and supporting families navigating divorce and remarriage.

5. Influence of Society and Culture:

- Gender Roles:

Societal expectations about gender roles can impact family dynamics, challenging traditional structures and redefining relationships. Illustrating this, let's consider the example of Shraddha and Shravan:

Shraddha and Shravan are a married couple in a traditional society where gender roles are well-defined. I

1. Division of Labor:

Gender roles often dictate specific family roles. For instance, Shravan is expected to be the primary breadwinner, while Shraddha takes on the role of a homemaker. This division can lead to a power imbalance, affecting financial decisions and household responsibilities.

2. Decision-Making:

Traditional gender roles may grant Shravan greater authority in family decisions, potentially marginalizing Shraddha's autonomy and input.

3. Emotional Expression:

Gender norms may influence how emotions are expressed. Societal pressure may lead Shravan to suppress emotions, while Shraddha may be encouraged to express herself more openly, creating potential misunderstandings.

4. Parenting Styles:

Gender roles may extend to parenting, with Shraddha expected to be nurturing and Shravan the disciplinarian. This can impact interactions with their children and shape their perception of gender roles.

5. Career Aspirations:

Gender roles can influence career choices, with Shravan pressured to pursue a demanding job as the primary provider, potentially sacrificing work-life balance. Shraddha's career ambitions may be limited due to societal expectations.

Overall, gender roles can create expectations influencing how Shraddha and Shravan interact, potentially leading to unequal power dynamics, limited fulfillment, and conflicts. Open communication is crucial for addressing and adapting to these dynamics.

- Cultural Norms:

Cultural values significantly shape family dynamics, impacting communication styles and expectations of piety or independence.

Examining Jeeva from Haryana and Tripti from Mumbai provides insights:

1. Gender Roles and Expectations:

In Haryana's patriarchal society, Jeeva may experience rigid gender roles, while Mumbai's cosmopolitan setting offers Tripti more diverse gender roles.

2. Arranged Marriage vs. Love Marriage:

Haryana sees a prevalence of arranged marriages, limiting Jeeva's choice, while Mumbai's love marriages afford individuals like Tripti more freedom.

3. Family Size and Structure:

Haryana tends to favor larger, extended families, fostering support but requiring conformity. Mumbai's urban setting may lead to smaller nuclear families with greater independence.

4. Social and Religious Traditions:

Rich agricultural traditions dominate Haryana, influencing family life. Mumbai's diversity results in a blend of cultural and religious practices.

5. Communication Styles:

Haryana emphasizes formal, hierarchical communication, while Mumbai encourages open and informal styles, allowing freer expression.

6. Educational and Career Goals:

Haryana's cultural norms may prioritize early marriage, potentially limiting educational and career aspirations. Mumbai's diverse culture allows more opportunities for education and career before marriage.

It's essential to recognize that family dynamics vary within regions and are influenced by factors like socioeconomic status and personal values. While cultural norms provide a framework, individuals like Jeeva and Tripti make choices based on unique circumstances and preferences.

6. Individual Personalities and Life Stages:

- Personality Differences:

Each family member's unique personality can either enhance or complicate relationships. For example, introverted and extroverted family members may have varying communication needs, impacting the overall dynamics. Recognizing and respecting these differences fosters a harmonious environment within the family.

- Life Stages:

Family relationships undergo transformations as individuals progress through different life stages. The dynamics between parents and adult children, for instance, differ significantly from those between grandparents and grandchildren. Understanding and adapting to these shifts are essential for maintaining healthy relationships across generations.

Family relationships are a dynamic interplay of individual personalities, societal norms, cultural influences, and life circumstances. These dynamics are not static; they change over time due to personal growth, evolving societal values, and changing life situations. Understanding and nurturing these relationships often require patience, open communication, and adaptability to navigate the complexities and nuances that arise.

Is Physical Intimacy the Most Important Aspect of a Romantic Relationship?

Physical intimacy can hold varying degrees of importance for couples in a healthy relationship, contributing to emotional connection, bonding, and overall satisfaction. However, its significance is subjective and differs among relationships. Some individuals prioritize physical intimacy as a means of expressing love and affection, while others may place greater importance on emotional connection, communication, or other facets of the relationship. Open and honest discussions about needs and preferences are crucial for ensuring mutual satisfaction and a sense of relationship health. The uniqueness of each relationship lies in the comfort and fulfilment experienced by both individuals.

1. Diverse Preferences:

Not everyone places the same value on physical intimacy or values it to the same degree. Some individuals may prioritize physical closeness as a means of expressing love and fostering emotional connection, while others may emphasize alternative forms of connection, such as emotional intimacy, communication, or shared activities.

Let's explore how diverse preferences in physical intimacy can be illustrated through case studies of different couples:

1. Shravan and Suhana:

Shravan and Suhana have been together for a few years. They prioritize emotional connection and communication in their relationship. While they enjoy physical intimacy, it's not a daily necessity for them. They find that cuddling and affectionate gestures, such as holding hands, are essential for their bond. Their intimacy preference is more emotionally driven.

2. Nisha and Nikunj:

Nisha and Nikunj are a passionate couple who prioritize physical intimacy in their relationship. They often express love through physical touch, affection, and intimacy. They believe that physical closeness is a vital part of their emotional connection, and they enjoy experimenting to keep their relationship exciting.

3. Rajesh and Ranjan:

Rajesh and Ranjan have an open and honest relationship. They have discussed their preferences and discovered they have different levels of desire for physical intimacy. While Rajesh enjoys it more frequently, Ranjan is content with occasional moments of closeness.

4. Deepti, Drishti, and Chetan:

Deepti, Drishti, and Chetan are in a polyamorous relationship. They've created a unique dynamic that allows them to explore varied preferences in physical intimacy. Each individual has different desires, and they communicate openly about their needs, ensuring everyone feels valued and satisfied.

2. Cultural and Personal Beliefs

Cultural backgrounds and personal beliefs can significantly influence the perception of physical intimacy within a relationship. Various cultures may place different emphasis on modesty and restraint, shaping individuals' attitudes and behaviours towards physical expression. Some cultures may adopt more permissive views, encouraging open displays of affection and intimacy, while others may prioritize privacy and discretion. Understanding and respecting these cultural nuances is crucial for couples to navigate their intimate dynamics in a way that aligns with their values and promotes a healthy, mutually satisfying relationship.

Case Study on Cultural and Personal Beliefs Affecting Physical Intimacy

Participants:

- Sandhya (Female, 28 years old)
- Shravan (Male, 30 years old)
- Mahit (Male, 35 years old)
- Antalya (Female, 32 years old)

Background:

Sandhya and Shravan are a couple from a conservative South Asian background. They were raised in families where discussions about physical intimacy were considered taboo, and premarital sex was strictly discouraged. They both adhere to traditional values and cultural norms. Mahit and Antalya, on the other hand, come from a Western background with more liberal views regarding physical intimacy and relationships.

Scenario 1: Sandhya and Shravan

Sandhya and Shravan have been in a committed relationship for five years. Despite their deep emotional connection, their conservative cultural beliefs significantly impact their physical intimacy. They find it challenging to openly discuss their desires and boundaries due to societal expectations. This has led to a lack of communication and understanding between them, resulting in infrequent physical intimacy and occasional tensions.

Scenario 2: Mahit and Antalya

Mahit and Antalya are a couple who share a more open and liberal view on physical intimacy. They communicate openly about their desires, preferences, and boundaries. Their personal beliefs align with their cultural background, which fosters a healthier approach to physical intimacy. They enjoy a satisfying and fulfilling physical relationship, as they don't face the same level of cultural restrictions as Sandhya and Shravan.

Implications and Discussion:

1. Cultural Beliefs: Cultural norms and values play a significant role in shaping individuals' views on physical intimacy. Sandhya and Shravan's conservative upbringing restricts their ability to explore their desires openly, leading to potential frustration and misunderstanding. Mahit and Antalya, however, have more freedom to express their desires and maintain a healthier physical connection.

2. Communication: Open communication is crucial in any relationship, but it can be hindered by cultural and personal beliefs. Sandhya and Shravan's inability to discuss their intimate needs stems from the fear of going against their cultural norms. In contrast, Mahit and Antalya's open communication stems from their cultural background, allowing them to nurture their physical connection.

3. Individuality: Personal beliefs can vary within the same cultural framework. While Sandhya and Shravan's cultural beliefs align with their reserved approach to physical intimacy, it is important to recognize that others from the same cultural background may have different perspectives. Similarly, Mahit and Antalya's liberal attitudes are consistent with their cultural background, but not all individuals from their culture may share these beliefs.

Cultural and personal beliefs can have a profound impact on physical intimacy within relationships. Understanding and respecting each other's backgrounds, beliefs, and values are essential for maintaining a healthy physical connection while navigating the complexities of cultural and personal influences.

3. Communication is Key: Open and honest communication is crucial in any relationship. Couples should discuss their expectations and boundaries regarding physical intimacy to ensure both partners are comfortable and on the same page.

In the case of Sunayana and Vartik, after open and honest communication, they realized they are not compatible when it comes to physical intimacy. However, they deeply love each other. In such situations, the solution may involve seeking couples counseling or therapy. Professional guidance can help them explore options, understand each other's needs, and find a compromise that works for both partners. If necessary, it may also lead to decisions about the future of their relationship, with the focus on maintaining love and respect while addressing differences in physical intimacy preferences.

Ending 1: Reimagining Intimacy

After their heartfelt conversation, Sunayana and Vartik recognized the depth of their emotional connection. While physical intimacy might not align, they decide to explore alternative ways to express their love. They begin to delve into hobbies they both enjoy, such as cooking, hiking, or dancing. Their bond strengthens as they invest more time in these shared activities, and they find new ways to experience closeness and passion in their relationship. Their love deepens as they embrace a more platonic but equally fulfilling form of intimacy.

Ending 2: Seeking Professional Guidance

Sunayana and Vartik's love for each other is undeniable, but their physical incompatibility remains a challenge. They opt to seek the guidance of a relationship counselor or therapist who can help them navigate this issue. Through therapy, they learn to understand each other's needs better and discover ways to compromise and enhance their physical connection. Over time, they find a middle ground that satisfies both of them, allowing their love to flourish in a fulfilling way.

Ending 3: Exploring Open Relationships

Recognizing their deep love for each other, Sunayana and Vartik have a candid conversation about their physical incompatibility and consider the option of opening their relationship. They agree to allow each other to explore physical intimacy with others while maintaining their emotional connection. This unconventional arrangement challenges their boundaries and trust but ultimately allows them to stay together and continue loving each other deeply. They find happiness in the unique dynamics of their open relationship.

Each of these endings has its merits, and the right solution depends on Sunayana and Vartik's values, preferences, and willingness to adapt to the complexities of their situation. The key is that they prioritize open communication, understanding, and respect for each other's needs to make their relationship work in the best way for them.

4. Changing Dynamics:

The importance of physical intimacy in a relationship can change over time. In the early stages of a relationship, physical attraction and the desire for closeness may be more prominent, while in long-term relationships, emotional connection and companionship can become equally or more important.

5. Health and Well-being:

Physical intimacy can have positive effects on a person's physical and mental well-being. It can reduce stress, increase feelings of closeness, and contribute to overall relationship satisfaction.

6. Balancing All Aspects:

A successful and fulfilling romantic relationship typically involves a balance of various forms of intimacy, including emotional, intellectual, and physical. Neglecting any one aspect can potentially lead to dissatisfaction.

Ultimately, the role of physical intimacy in a relationship is a highly individual matter, and what matters most is that both partners feel comfortable, respected, and fulfilled in their relationship. It's essential for couples to have ongoing discussions about their needs and desires to ensure a healthy and mutually satisfying connection.

Sometimes Relationships stink. But why?

Miscommunication in relationships can lead to misunderstandings, conflicts, and strained connections. Here are some day-to-day examples to illustrate this:

Texting Misinterpretations:

When one partner sends a text message that's meant to be light-hearted, but the other interprets it as sarcasm or criticism. This can quickly escalate into an argument due to the lack of tone and context in text messages.

Nishant and Shruti were a happy couple deeply in love, but their relationship took an unexpected turn due to a texting misinterpretation. One evening, Nishant sent a message to Shruti saying, "Can we talk later? Something important to discuss."

Shruti, already having a stressful day, misread his message as a sign of trouble. She replied, "What's wrong? Is something bad happening?" Worried, she imagined all sorts of worst-case scenarios.

Nishant, on the other hand, meant to discuss something trivial, like dinner plans. But seeing Shruti's response, he felt overwhelmed and assumed she must be angry at him for some reason.

Their miscommunications continued, and each text made things worse. Eventually, they both started to read negative intentions into each other's messages, and their relationship became strained.

One day, they decided to meet in person to address the growing tension. As they talked, they realized the misinterpretations and misunderstandings that had arisen from their texts. They both laughed at the absurdity of it all and promised to communicate better in the future.

Nishant and Shruti faced a strain in their relationship due to a texting misinterpretation. Nishant's innocent message about discussing dinner plans turned into a series of misunderstandings, escalating tensions. They later realized the importance of open and honest communication, especially in the age of texting.

Assuming Instead of Asking:

One partner assumes the other's preferences without confirming. For instance, assuming that the other person wants to eat out when they actually prefer a quiet night at home. This can lead to unmet expectations.

Once upon a time in a quaint little village, there lived a couple named Raman and Rama. They had been together for many years and had always shared a loving and healthy relationship. However, as time passed, a subtle shift began to occur.

Raman and Rama were both hardworking individuals, and they both held full-time jobs to support their family. One day, Rama noticed that Raman seemed distant and preoccupied. Instead of asking him what was bothering him, she assumed that he was just tired from work.

Days turned into weeks, and Raman's distance continued to grow. He, on the other hand, noticed that Rama had been spending more time with her friends and less with him. Instead of talking to her about his feelings, he assumed that she was simply enjoying her social life.

As the months went by, their assumptions started to erode their trust and communication. Rama began to feel neglected and unappreciated, while Raman felt increasingly isolated and misunderstood. They both carried their silent grievances, assuming that the other person would eventually notice and address their concerns.

One evening, their pent-up frustration finally reached a breaking point. Rama came home late after a night out with her friends, and Raman was waiting for her with a cold silence. Instead of talking things out, their anger led to a heated argument. They accused each other of neglecting the relationship and not caring anymore.

The argument left both Raman and Rama hurt and in tears. They realized that their assumptions had poisoned their once-healthy relationship. The next day, they decided to sit down and have an open and honest conversation about their feelings and concerns. As they talked, they realized that their assumptions had been completely wrong.

Raman had been preoccupied with a work-related project that was causing stress, and he hadn't intended to distance himself from Rama. Rama, on the other hand, had been spending more time with her friends to fill the void left by Raman's emotional withdrawal.

Through their conversation, they realized the importance of communication and not making assumptions. They pledged to be more open with each other and to discuss their feelings and concerns rather than jumping to conclusions. Over time, they worked to rebuild their trust and love for one another, and their relationship became stronger than ever before.

Raman and Rama's relationship hit a rough patch when they started assuming each other's preferences without confirmation. Unspoken assumptions led to misunderstandings and a breakdown in trust. A face-to-face conversation helped them understand the importance of open communication and addressing concerns.

Interrupting and Not Listening:

Nandita sits on the couch, looking anxious. Nishan is engrossed in his phone.

NANDITA

(trying to get Nishan's attention)

Nishan, can we talk? I really need to tell you something that's been bothering me at work.

NISHAN

(disinterested)

Yeah, sure, go ahead.

Nandita takes a deep breath.

NANDITA

(worried)

Well, you know that new project I've been working on, right? It's been really stressful lately. The deadlines are tight, and I feel like I'm drowning in tasks. Plus, my boss...

Before Nandita can finish her sentence, Nishan's phone pings, and he immediately starts texting.

NANDITA

(irritated)

Nishan, can you please put your phone down and listen to me? This is important!

Nishan briefly looks up from his phone.

NISHAN

(absentmindedly)

Sorry, go on.

Nandita continues, frustrated.

NANDITA

(rapidly)

So, my boss keeps piling on more work, and my coworker, Sarah, always takes credit for my ideas. It's like I'm invisible there.

NISHAN

(distracted)

That's tough, babe. But you know, work can be like that sometimes.

Nandita sighs, feeling dismissed.

NANDITA

(annoyed)

It's not just "like that" this time, Nishan. I feel overwhelmed, and I thought you'd be the one I could talk to about it.

Nishan finally looks up, seeming a bit more attentive.

NISHAN

(sincere)

I'm sorry, Nandita. I didn't mean to brush it off. I'm here for you. Tell me more.

Nandita, now calmer, starts sharing her frustrations and concerns about her work situation with Nishan, grateful that he's finally listening.

Nandita felt unheard when Nishan constantly interrupted their conversation, engrossed in his phone. This led to frustration and a breakdown in communication. When Nishan finally listened attentively, their relationship improved, emphasizing the importance of active listening.

Non-Verbal Cues:

Misunderstanding non-verbal cues such as body language and facial expressions. For example, misinterpreting a sigh as annoyance when it might actually signify tiredness.

Expecting Mind Reading:

Expecting your partner to know what you need or want without explicitly communicating it. For example, feeling hurt because your partner didn't plan a surprise for your birthday when you never mentioned wanting one.

Nishi and Nishant had been dating for a year, and their relationship was mostly blissful. They shared many common interests and cherished their time together. However, there was one recurring issue that occasionally caused tension: their unspoken expectations of mind reading.

One evening, Nishi was feeling particularly down after a tough day at work. She expected Nishant to know this without her saying a word. As they sat on the couch, she sighed deeply, hoping he would notice and comfort her. But Nishant, engrossed in his own thoughts, failed to pick up on her distress.

Nishi's frustration grew, and she eventually snapped, "Why can't you see that I'm upset?" Nishant, caught off guard, tried to console her, but the damage was done. Nishi felt let down, and Nishant felt unfairly blamed.

A few weeks later, it was Nishant's turn to feel misunderstood. He had been planning a surprise anniversary dinner for Nishi, hoping she would realize he'd put in a lot of effort to make it special. But as the day approached, Nishi seemed oblivious to his hints and subtle clues, causing Nishant to become increasingly agitated.

When the anniversary finally arrived, Nishi was genuinely surprised by the effort Nishant had put into the dinner. However, she couldn't help but sense his frustration earlier, leading to a tense start to their special evening.

These incidents continued to mount over time. Nishi and Nishant realized that expecting mind-reading was causing more harm than good in their relationship. They decided to have an open and honest conversation about their feelings and expectations. They acknowledged that while they knew each other well, they couldn't always guess each other's thoughts and emotions.

From that point on, they started expressing their feelings and needs more explicitly, which brought them closer together. They learned that clear communication was the key to understanding each other's needs and maintaining a healthy, harmonious relationship. While they occasionally slipped back into old habits, they now had a strong foundation to address these issues and prevent them from causing a rift in their relationship.

Nishi and Nishant faced challenges when they expected the other to intuitively understand their needs. Clear communication became the key to resolving issues and preventing misunderstandings.

Differing Communication Styles: Couples with contrasting communication styles may face frustration. Understanding and respecting each other's coping mechanisms can alleviate tension.

One person prefers to talk things out immediately when conflicts arise, while the other needs time alone to process their thoughts. This can lead to frustration if they don't understand each other's coping mechanisms.

Dhara and Aakash, a couple with advanced degrees and successful careers, had built a life together over their four years of marriage. Their journey, however, was marred by a recurring issue - their divergent approaches to conflict resolution.

Aakash, being a proactive communicator, believed in addressing conflicts head-on. His rationale was grounded in a desire for swift resolution, thinking that it would prevent lingering resentment. He saw open communication as the key to a healthy relationship and believed that addressing issues promptly was a sign of commitment.

On the other hand, Dhara, despite her intellectual prowess, had a habit of withdrawing when faced with conflict. She sought solace in temporary isolation, allowing herself time to cool down before engaging in a conversation. Her perspective was rooted in the belief that discussing issues in the heat of the moment only fueled emotional turmoil and hindered productive dialogue.

As the years passed, this divergence in their conflict resolution styles started taking a toll on their relationship. Aakash felt frustrated by what he perceived as Dhara's avoidance, interpreting it as a lack of commitment or interest in resolving issues. Dhara, in turn, felt overwhelmed by Aakash's insistence on addressing conflicts immediately, often feeling cornered and unable to express her thoughts effectively.

Their differences became increasingly apparent, turning what could have been minor disagreements into major sources of tension. The emotional distance created by these clashes began to erode the foundation of their once-strong bond.

To bridge this gap, Dhara and Aakash needed to recognize and respect each other's preferred methods of conflict resolution. They could establish a middle ground by agreeing on a timeline for discussions – perhaps a commitment from Aakash to allow Dhara the time she needed before initiating conversations. Equally, Dhara could make an effort to communicate her need for space and assure Aakash that she valued resolving conflicts as much as he did.

The key was for them to acknowledge that their distinct approaches weren't indicative of a lack of love or commitment. Instead, these differences could be seen as complementary if they learned to navigate them together. By finding common ground and embracing each other's perspectives, Dhara and Aakash could transform their conflict resolution dynamics, fostering a healthier and more understanding relationship.

Mixed Messages: Giving mixed signals can lead to confusion and misinterpretation. Open communication is crucial to understanding each other's true feelings.

For example, saying "I'm fine" when you're actually upset, expecting your partner to discern your true feelings.

Suman and Samrat, inseparable since their college days, had a friendship that bloomed like a cherished garden. Yet, as time passed, subtle miscommunications began to cast shadows on their once unbreakable bond.

Occasion 1: The Birthday Surprise

Suman, excitedly planning a surprise birthday celebration for Samrat, began spending more time with another friend, Priya, to organize the event. Samrat, unaware of the surprise, interpreted Suman's sudden closeness with Priya as a sign of shifting priorities. Feeling neglected, he started distancing himself.

Resolution:

Suman, sensing Samrat's discomfort, decided to unveil the surprise earlier. She explained her intentions, emphasizing that their friendship remained a priority. Samrat, touched by the effort and honesty, realized the misunderstanding and embraced Suman's gesture with gratitude.

Occasion 2: The Job Promotion

When Samrat landed a significant job promotion, he hesitated to share the news with Suman, fearing it might seem like bragging. Meanwhile, Suman, unaware of Samrat's promotion, felt left out of a significant aspect of his life.

Resolution:

Samrat eventually mustered the courage to share his achievement with Suman. Rather than feeling neglected,

Suman was genuinely thrilled for her friend. They acknowledged the importance of sharing their successes and challenges, ensuring transparency in their friendship.

Occasion 3: The Unreturned Calls

As life grew busier, Suman found herself unable to return Samrat's calls promptly. Samrat, interpreting the delays as a lack of interest, started questioning the strength of their bond.

Resolution:

Recognizing the strain, Suman initiated an honest conversation about her time constraints. She reassured Samrat that their friendship remained invaluable, proposing a more structured approach to their communication. Samrat appreciated Suman's openness and agreed to a more understanding and flexible communication style.

In each instance, Suman and Samrat confronted the misinterpretations and mixed signals threatening their friendship. By fostering open communication, they learned to navigate life's changes together. These challenges served as opportunities to strengthen their bond, reinforcing the resilience of their beautiful friendship. Through shared laughter and heartfelt conversations, Suman and Samrat ensured that their connection flourished, free from the shadows of misunderstood messages.

Assuming Similar Priorities: Believing partners share the same priorities without discussing them can lead to conflicts over issues like finances, career goals, or family planning.

Scenario 1: The Anniversary Dilemma

Anuj, focused on family, planned an intimate anniversary celebration. Antra, immersed in her career, committed to an important work event on the same day. Anuj felt neglected, assuming they shared the same priorities, while Antra felt pressured to balance work and personal life.

Anuj and antra

Handling the Situation:

An honest conversation is crucial. Anuj and Antra should openly express their expectations and understand the differing importance they place on family and career. Finding compromises, such as rescheduling celebrations or Antra setting boundaries at work, can help strike a balance.

Scenario 2: Quality Time vs. Work Commitments

Anuj yearned for quality time with Antra, who consistently brought work stress home. Antra, thinking they shared the same work ethic, believed her dedication to career was understood. This misalignment caused emotional distance.

Handling the Situation:

Anuj and Antra should discuss their expectations regarding personal and professional time. Establishing designated moments for undistracted quality time and acknowledging the significance of Antra's career commitments can help maintain equilibrium.

Scenario 3: Future Planning

Anuj, envisioning a family-centric future, assumed Antra held similar aspirations. Antra, driven by career goals, hadn't considered the extent of Anuj's expectations. The revelation caused friction and uncertainty about their shared future.

Handling the Situation:

An open dialogue about long-term plans is essential. Anuj and Antra should discuss their individual goals, expectations, and compromises. Understanding each other's perspectives will help align their future visions and reduce potential conflicts.

Scenario 4: Emotional Support vs. Professional Achievements

During a challenging time for Anuj, Antra's preoccupation with work left him feeling unsupported. Antra, assuming Anuj's resilience, underestimated the emotional toll of his struggles.

Handling the Situation:

Expressing emotional needs is crucial. Anuj and Antra should communicate openly about their expectations for support during difficult times. Balancing emotional support and professional pursuits is a delicate dance, requiring mutual understanding and compromise.

Overall Resolution:

To salvage their relationship, Anuj and Antra need to embrace their differences and communicate effectively. Recognizing and respecting each other's priorities is vital. Establishing clear boundaries, discussing future plans openly, and finding compromises will help them navigate the intricacies of their individual priorities and foster a healthier, more understanding relationship.

Overusing Technology: Spending excessive time on screens instead of engaging in face-to-face conversations can create feelings of neglect and disconnection.

Sudha Sushant and technology

Sudha, once a lively and vibrant soul, found herself trapped in the echoes of a joint conservative family after marriage. Longing for the familiar warmth of her family and friends, she felt like a caged bird stripped of its song. The joy that once radiated from her eyes started to dim, replaced by the loneliness of unspoken desires.

Sushant, her husband, unintentionally contributed to her isolation. While physically present at home, his attention was perpetually diverted – absorbed in his phone or the captivating glow of Netflix. Sudha's attempts to initiate conversations often met with distracted nods or fleeting glances, leaving her emotionally stranded in the vast emptiness of their shared space.

As the emotional distance widened, Sudha's heartache became unbearable. She yearned for a connection that transcended the superficial coexistence they found themselves in. Nights echoed with the silence of unspoken words, and Sudha's spirit, once as free as a bird, felt bound by the chains of unexpressed longing.

One day, unable to carry the weight of her unspoken sorrow any longer, Sudha mustered the strength to have a candid conversation with Sushant. Tears flowed as she poured out the loneliness that had become her constant companion. Sushant, initially surprised by the depth of Sudha's emotions, was struck by the realization of the chasm that had silently grown between them.

In that poignant moment, the couple faced a crossroads – a choice between accepting the status quo or embarking on a journey to rediscover the love that brought them together. Sushant, awakened by Sudha's vulnerability, recognized the significance of their connection. In a sincere effort to rebuild their relationship, he pledged to be present not just physically but emotionally.

They started by establishing dedicated times for genuine conversations, free from distractions. Sushant put away his phone during those moments, choosing Sudha over the digital noise. Slowly, the walls that separated them began to crumble, replaced by a bridge of shared laughter, tears, and rediscovered affection.

Through open communication, they tackled the issues that had pushed Sudha to the brink. Sudha, feeling heard and valued, found solace in Sushant's renewed commitment. Their journey, though challenging, became a testament to the transformative power of vulnerability, communication, and a shared willingness to rebuild what had almost been lost.

In the end, Sudha's decision to confront the silence and Sushant's dedication to breaking free from distraction became the foundation on which they rebuilt their relationship, stronger and more resilient than ever before.

Overloading with Information: Sharing too much information can overwhelm the other person, leading to disinterest. Clear and concise communication is essential.

Unrealistic Expectations: Expecting perfection, constant happiness, or unchanging appearances can lead to disappointment. Communicating about realistic expectations is crucial for a healthy relationship.

Unrealistic expectations in relationships can strain them and lead to disappointment. Here are some day-to-day examples:

1. Constant Happiness: Expecting your partner to always make you happy, ignoring the fact that everyone has ups and downs.

2. Perfect Communication: Believing that your partner should always understand your thoughts and feelings without any effort.

3. Exclusivity of Time: Thinking your partner should spend every free moment with you, neglecting their need for personal space and other responsibilities.

4. Financial Dependency: Expecting your partner to provide for you entirely, rather than sharing financial responsibilities equally.

5. Mind Reading: Assuming your partner should intuitively know what you want without you expressing your desires.

6. Unchanging Appearance: Believing your partner should always look the same as when you first met, despite the natural aging process.

7. Solving All Problems: Expecting your partner to solve all of your life's issues, instead of seeking professional help when needed.

8. Constant Romance: Thinking that the initial passion of a relationship should never fade, rather than understanding that love evolves.

9. Perfect Compatibility: Believing that you and your partner should have no differences or disagreements, which is unrealistic in any relationship.

10. Never Making Mistakes: Holding your partner to an impossible standard where they can't make any mistakes or have flaws.

It's important to recognize and communicate about these unrealistic expectations to build healthier and more sustainable relationships.

3. Lack of Trust: Trust issues can erode the foundation of a relationship and create feelings of insecurity.

Lack of trust in a relationship can manifest in various ways through day-to-day examples. Here are some scenarios to illustrate this:

1. **Communication Secrecy:** Partners may hide their messages, emails, or phone calls, creating suspicion. For instance, if someone constantly locks their phone or deletes messages to keep their communication hidden.

2. **Broken Promises:** If one partner repeatedly fails to follow through on commitments, such as promising to help with chores but not doing so, it erodes trust over time.

3. **Jealousy and Suspicion:** Unwarranted jealousy or suspicion can lead to constant questioning and monitoring of each other's activities, causing stress and insecurity.

4. **Lack of Transparency:** Keeping financial matters hidden, like hidden bank accounts or undisclosed spending, can create a significant lack of trust in a relationship.

5. **Infidelity:** The most significant breach of trust is infidelity, where one partner engages in a romantic or sexual relationship outside the partnership.

6. **Inconsistent Behavior:** Sudden changes in behavior, mood swings, or inconsistency in one's actions can lead a partner to question the sincerity of their intentions.

7. **Withholding Affection:** When one partner withholds affection, emotional support, or intimacy without valid reasons, it can signal a lack of trust or emotional disconnect.

8. **Gossip and Betrayal:** Sharing personal information or sensitive stories about your partner with friends or family can breach their trust.

9. **Microaggressions:** Small but hurtful comments or actions, like sarcastic remarks or belittling gestures, can accumulate and erode trust.

10. **Past Deception:** If someone has lied or deceived their partner in the past, it can take a long time to rebuild trust, as the memory of that betrayal lingers.

In each of these examples, trust is compromised, and if not addressed, it can lead to significant issues in the relationship. Building and maintaining trust is essential for a healthy and fulfilling partnership.

4. Differences in Values or Goals: When partners have vastly different values or long-term goals, it can create tension and conflict.

Differences in values or goals can significantly impact relationships. Here are some day-to-day examples to elaborate on this:

1. **Career Ambitions**: Imagine one partner values a high-powered career with long working hours and is focused on climbing the corporate ladder, while the other prioritizes work-life balance and spending quality time with family. This misalignment in career goals can lead to conflicts and strain the relationship.

2. **Financial Priorities**: Suppose one person values saving and investing for the future, while the other enjoys spending money on immediate experiences and luxury items. This difference in financial goals can lead to disagreements over budgeting, saving, and lifestyle choices.

3. **Religious Beliefs**: Consider a couple where one partner is deeply religious and attends religious services regularly, while the other is not religious and prefers secular activities. These differing beliefs can create tension regarding how they

spend their weekends or raise children with conflicting value systems.

4. **Health and Fitness**: Picture a scenario where one partner is committed to a healthy lifestyle, prioritizing exercise and a nutritious diet, while the other is less concerned about health and indulges in unhealthy habits. This can lead to friction around meal choices, exercise routines, and overall well-being.

5. **Family Planning**: Think about a couple where one person desires to have children soon, while the other wants to delay parenthood to pursue personal goals or travel. This variance in family planning can lead to emotional stress and decisions about the timing of starting a family.

6. **Communication Styles**: Suppose one partner values open and direct communication, while the other tends to be more reserved and avoids confrontations. This difference in communication styles can lead to misunderstandings and difficulty resolving conflicts.

7. **Political Beliefs**: Imagine a situation where one partner is politically liberal and the other is conservative. Their contrasting political values can lead to heated discussions and differences in how they approach societal issues.

8. **Travel Preferences**: Consider a couple where one partner loves adventure travel and exploring new places, while the other prefers relaxing beach vacations. These differences in travel preferences can affect vacation planning and the overall satisfaction of travel experiences.

In each of these scenarios, it's essential for individuals in the relationship to communicate openly, respect each other's values and goals, and find compromises or common ground to maintain a healthy and fulfilling partnership. If left unaddressed, significant differences in values or goals can strain relationships and potentially lead to their dissolution.

Health and fitness play a significant role in relationships, contributing to overall well-being and the quality of interpersonal connections. Here are some day-to-day examples of how health and fitness can impact relationships:

1. **Shared Activities**: Engaging in physical activities together, such as jogging, hiking, or dancing, can strengthen the bond between partners. It provides an opportunity to spend quality time together, encourages teamwork, and promotes a healthier lifestyle for both individuals.

2. **Healthy Eating Habits**: Preparing and enjoying nutritious meals together can enhance a couple's connection. Planning and cooking meals that prioritize fresh ingredients and balanced nutrition can be a collaborative and enjoyable experience.

3. **Emotional Well-being**: Regular exercise releases endorphins, which can improve mood and reduce stress. When both partners prioritize their fitness, they are better equipped to handle daily stressors and conflicts in a more constructive manner, leading to a more harmonious relationship.

4. **Accountability and Motivation**: When partners support each other in achieving fitness goals, it fosters a sense of accountability. This mutual encouragement can lead to higher adherence to exercise routines and healthier lifestyle choices.

5. **Increased Attraction**: Staying fit and healthy can enhance physical attraction, which can positively impact the romantic aspect of a relationship. Feeling good about one's body and health can boost self-esteem and confidence, making one more desirable to their partner.

6. **Longevity and Future Planning**: A focus on health and fitness can lead to discussions about long-term planning, such as retirement goals and aging gracefully together. Couples who prioritize their health tend to think more about their future well-being.

7. **Role Modeling**: If there are children in the relationship, demonstrating a commitment to health and fitness sets a positive example. Children are more likely to adopt healthy habits when they see their parents valuing and prioritizing them.

8. **Conflict Resolution**: Engaging in physical activities can serve as a healthy outlet for tension and frustration. It can also offer a buffer against relationship conflicts, as exercise is known to improve cognitive function and emotional regulation.

9. **Increased Energy and Productivity**: Improved fitness levels can lead to increased energy and productivity throughout the day. This can benefit the relationship by allowing partners to share responsibilities more effectively and enjoy leisure activities together.

10. **Support during Health Challenges**: In times of illness or health challenges, a partner's support and understanding become crucial. Having a foundation of health-consciousness can make it easier to navigate such difficulties together and provide emotional strength.

In summary, health and fitness are integral components of a strong and vibrant relationship. When both partners prioritize their well-being and incorporate healthy habits into their daily lives, it can lead to improved communication, emotional closeness, and a shared commitment to a fulfilling, active, and joyful life together.

6. **Philanthropy**:

- Individual G is committed to social causes and regularly volunteers at local shelters and donates to charities.

- Individual H focuses on personal financial stability and rarely contributes to charitable organizations.

These examples illustrate how differences in values or goals can influence daily choices and behaviors, leading to diverse lifestyles and priorities among individuals. It's important to recognize and respect these differences to promote understanding and harmony in society.

Philanthropy can sometimes be a source of relationship problems, both in personal relationships and within the context of organizations or communities. Here's an elaboration on this issue with an example:

1. **Divergent Philanthropic Values:** In personal relationships, individuals may have different philanthropic values and priorities. For example, one partner may be passionate about environmental causes and want to donate a significant portion of their income to related charities, while the other may be more focused on supporting local community initiatives. This misalignment can lead to conflicts if not addressed openly.

2. **Financial Strain:** Generosity in philanthropy often involves giving away a portion of one's income or assets. In some cases, this can strain a relationship when the giving partner's contributions significantly affect the couple's financial stability. Disagreements may arise over how much is appropriate to give, potentially leading to financial stress and tension in the relationship.

3. **Different Approaches to Giving:** People have varying approaches to philanthropy, such as hands-on volunteering,

making financial donations, or using their professional skills for charitable work. If one person in a relationship prefers a more active involvement in philanthropy, while the other prefers to simply donate money, it can create misunderstandings and disagreements.

Lack of Trust: Trust issues manifest in various ways, from communication secrecy to broken promises or infidelity. Rebuilding trust requires open communication and understanding.

Differences in Values or Goals: Varied priorities, such as career ambitions, financial habits, or family planning, can create tension. Open communication and compromise are vital to navigate these differences.

Health and Fitness in Relationships: Prioritizing health and fitness together can strengthen the bond between partners, improve emotional well-being, and foster mutual support.

3. Philanthropy:

Individual G is committed to social causes and regularly volunteers at local shelters and donates to charities. Individual H focuses on personal financial stability and rarely contributes to charitable organizations. These examples illustrate how differences in values or goals can influence daily choices and behaviors, leading to diverse lifestyles and priorities among individuals. It's important to recognize and respect these differences to promote understanding and harmony in society.

Philanthropy can sometimes be a source of relationship problems, both in personal relationships and within the context of organizations or communities. Here's an elaboration on this issue with an example:

Divergent Philanthropic Values: In personal relationships, individuals may have different philanthropic values and priorities. For example, one partner may be passionate about environmental causes and want to donate a significant portion of their income to related charities, while the other may be more focused on supporting local community initiatives. This misalignment can lead to conflicts if not addressed openly.

Financial Strain: Generosity in philanthropy often involves giving away a portion of one's income or assets. In some cases, this can strain a relationship when the giving partner's contributions significantly affect the couple's financial stability. Disagreements may arise over how much is appropriate to give, potentially leading to financial stress and tension in the relationship.

Different Approaches to Giving: People have varying approaches to philanthropy, such as hands-on volunteering, making financial donations, or using their professional skills for charitable work. If one person in a relationship prefers a more active involvement in philanthropy, while the other prefers to simply donate money, it can create misunderstandings and disagreements.

Social Expectations: In certain social circles or communities, there may be expectations or pressure to participate in philanthropic activities or donate to specific causes. This can lead to conflicts if one person feels compelled to give in order to fit in, while the other believes that charitable actions should be based on personal values and not external pressures.

Example:

Imagine a married couple, Alex and Taylor. Alex is a successful tech entrepreneur with a strong passion for global health initiatives and wants to donate a significant portion of their wealth to support medical research in developing countries. Taylor, on the other hand, works in a local nonprofit organization that focuses on homelessness in their city and believes that their philanthropic efforts should be directed toward immediate community needs.

As Alex starts allocating a substantial part of their income to international health organizations, Taylor becomes increasingly concerned about their own nonprofit's financial struggles. This difference in philanthropic priorities and the financial strain it puts on their relationship causes tension between them. They have difficulty reconciling their individual passions and values, leading to arguments and a sense of disconnection.

In this example, the differing philanthropic priorities of Alex and Taylor have become a relationship problem. To address it, they would need open and empathetic communication, compromise, and potentially finding ways to support both global health and local community initiatives without compromising their financial stability or the harmony of their relationship.

External Stressors:

External factors like work, financial problems, or family issues can spill over into a relationship and make it challenging.

External stressors in relationships refer to outside factors or circumstances that can place strain on the relationship and potentially lead to issues or conflicts. These stressors can come from various sources and impact the relationship in different ways. Here are some common external stressors in relationships with examples:

Financial Stress: Money-related issues are a significant external stressor. For instance, if one partner loses their job, it can create financial instability and lead to conflicts over budgeting, spending habits, or bills.

Once upon a time, in the quaint town of Serenity, Naman and Nayonika were the epitome of a happy family. Blessed with two children, Aarav and Anika, they reveled in the simple joys of life. Naman, a dedicated software engineer, provided a comfortable life for his family. Their home resonated with laughter, warmth, and an air of contentment.

However, life took an unexpected turn when Naman lost his job due to a sudden downturn in the tech industry. The pink slip shattered the tranquility of their existence, replacing it with the looming clouds of uncertainty. Determined to weather the storm together, Naman and Nayonika huddled to discuss their next steps.

The initial months were challenging, with savings dwindling and the burden of monthly expenses weighing heavily on their shoulders. EMI reminders and children's school fees became persistent echoes of their financial predicament. Naman, despite his best efforts, struggled to secure a new job, intensifying the strain on their relationship.

In the face of adversity, Nayonika, a skilled event planner, took on extra projects to ease the financial burden. Yet, the relentless pressure seeped into their home, sowing seeds of frustration and discontent. The couple, once united in joy, found themselves entangled in arguments fueled by the stress of unpaid bills and unmet expectations.

As the financial stress reached its peak, a pivotal moment arrived. Naman, feeling defeated, contemplated his worth and role as the provider. Nayonika, torn between her responsibilities and the emotional distance that had crept into their relationship, yearned for the days when their love was unburdened by financial worries.

Positive Ending:

In a moment of clarity, Naman and Nayonika decided to confront their challenges head-on. They attended financial counseling sessions, established a realistic budget, and communicated openly about their fears and aspirations. Naman, buoyed by Nayonika's unwavering support, diversified his job search, eventually securing a position in a growing startup. The couple's shared resilience not only mended the financial wounds but also deepened their emotional connection. Together, they emerged from the storm, stronger, and more attuned to each other's needs.

Negative Ending:

Regrettably, the mounting tension proved insurmountable for Naman and Nayonika. The constant financial strain eroded the foundation of their relationship. Unable to find common ground, they drifted apart emotionally. The once vibrant home now echoed with silence, punctuated only by the occasional argument. Faced with the harsh reality of their situation, Naman and Nayonika, with heavy hearts, chose to part ways. The echoes of their shattered dreams served as a somber reminder of how financial stress, if left unaddressed, can unravel even the most loving partnerships.

Family and In-Law Issues: Conflicts with extended family members, such as parents or in-laws, can affect a relationship. For example, if one partner feels that the other's family is overly involved or critical, it can lead to tension.

Vandana and Abhinav were a couple deeply in love, navigating the complexities of married life. Vandana, being the eldest of two sisters, found herself shouldering the responsibility of taking care of her aged mother after her father's demise. This commitment created an unintentional stress point in her relationship with Abhinav and his parents.

As Vandana devoted more time to her mother's needs, Abhinav and his parents started feeling neglected. They perceived Vandana's attention toward her mother as excessive, often leading to misunderstandings and tension in their family life.

The real issue stemmed from a lack of communication. Vandana was torn between her duties as a daughter and her responsibilities as a wife. Abhinav, in turn, felt overlooked and struggled to comprehend the emotional burden Vandana carried.

The turning point came when Vandana and Abhinav had an open and honest conversation about their feelings. Vandana explained the cultural and familial expectations placed upon her

as the eldest daughter. Abhinav, in turn, expressed his need for more attention and quality time in their relationship.

Together, they found a middle ground. Vandana involved Abhinav in the care of her mother, helping him understand the challenges she faced. This not only brought Abhinav closer to Vandana's family but also made him appreciate the effort Vandana put into caring for her mother.

To address the broader issue, Vandana and Abhinav started scheduling quality time for themselves, ensuring that their relationship remained a priority. They also communicated openly about their feelings and concerns, fostering a deeper understanding of each other's needs.

Vandana wasn't wrong in taking care of her aged mother; it was the lack of communication and understanding that caused the strain. The resolution came through empathy, compromise, and a commitment to maintaining a healthy balance between familial responsibilities and the needs of the marriage.

The solution to such common problems in married couples lies in effective communication and mutual understanding. It's crucial for partners to express their feelings, listen to each other, and find compromises that accommodate both individual and shared responsibilities. Balancing familial duties with the needs of the marriage requires constant effort and a willingness to adapt.

Work-related Stress: High-pressure jobs or long working hours can lead to stress in a relationship. If one partner is constantly stressed from work and brings that stress home, it can affect their emotional availability and communication with their partner.

Pankaj and Prema, once deeply in love, found their relationship strained as work-related pressures escalated. Long hours at the office became the norm, leaving little time for shared moments. The constant stress and deadlines led to communication breakdowns, turning their home into a silent battleground. Their once vibrant connection eroded under the weight of professional demands, leaving them yearning for the simplicity of the past.

Recognizing the toll work had taken on their relationship, Pankaj and Prema decided to prioritize their connection. They established dedicated "unplugged" time, free from work discussions. Communication improved as they openly shared their feelings and concerns. Together, they set boundaries on work hours and committed to rejuvenating their bond. Seeking support from each other, they navigated the challenges as a team, ultimately rediscovering the strength of their relationship amid life's demands.

Health Problems: Health issues, either of one of the partners or a family member, can be a significant stressor. For instance, if one partner has a chronic illness, it can place emotional and financial burdens on the relationship.

Pallavi and Prashant faced a daunting challenge after a decade of marital bliss: Prashant was diagnosed with severe kidney issues, threatening their family's stability. Undeterred, Pallavi, driven by love, shouldered the financial burden by dedicating extra hours to her coaching center and engaging in online work.

Meanwhile, Prashant, recognizing the importance of his health, opted for less strenuous projects and focused on spending quality time with their two daughters. Together, they navigated the turbulent waters of health concerns while fortifying their family bonds.

As the years passed, their resilience paid off. Their daughters, now grown and studying abroad, thrived in their pursuits. Pallavi, unwavering in her commitment, not only ensured their financial stability but also pursued her dreams. She traveled the world for work, sometimes with Prashant, sometimes solo, proving that love and determination can conquer even the most challenging obstacles.

In the face of adversity, Pallavi and Prashant not only preserved their relationship but also flourished individually. Today, they stand as proud parents, their journey serving as a testament to the power of love, perseverance, and unwavering support.

Parenting Challenges: Raising children can be stressful, especially if there are differences in parenting styles or if one partner feels overwhelmed. Disagreements about discipline, education, or childcare can strain the relationship.

Long-Distance Relationships: Physical separation due to work or other commitments can create stress. Maintaining emotional connection and trust in a long-distance relationship can be challenging.

In a world connected by screens, Nitya and Naman embarked on a challenging long-distance relationship, battling time zones and technological glitches. Despite the miles, their love thrived initially.

Ending 1 - Triumph over Trials:

They faced communication hurdles and misunderstandings, but their commitment prevailed. Late-night video calls, surprise virtual dates, and handwritten letters kept the flame alive. They learned to trust and appreciate each other's independence. The challenges strengthened their bond, and after two years, Nitya and Naman closed the distance, realizing that love can conquer miles.

Ending 2 - Drifting Apart:

Over time, the distance took its toll. Trust issues crept in, and misunderstandings festered. The lack of physical presence led to a growing emotional gap. Despite efforts, their connection weakened. Eventually, Nitya and Naman acknowledged the strain and chose different paths, realizing that sometimes love isn't enough to bridge the miles.

Vandana and Abhinav faced a challenge that many couples encounter in their journey – balancing familial responsibilities with the needs of their marriage. As Vandana devoted herself to caring for her aged mother, Abhinav felt neglected and yearned for more attention in their relationship. Their solution came through open communication, understanding, and compromise.

In the face of Vandana's family obligations, Abhinav joined her in caring for her mother, bridging the gap between their lives. This not only strengthened his connection with Vandana's family but also fostered a deeper appreciation for Vandana's efforts. The couple then took deliberate steps to schedule quality time for themselves, ensuring that their relationship remained a priority amid familial duties.

The lesson from Vandana and Abhinav's story is clear: effective communication and mutual understanding are crucial for navigating common challenges in married life. By expressing their feelings, listening to each other, and finding compromises, couples can strike a balance between individual and shared responsibilities.

Work-related stress can also take a toll on relationships,

1. High-pressure jobs or long working hours can lead to stress in a relationship. If one partner is constantly stressed from work and brings that stress home, it can affect their emotional availability and communication with their partner.

Pankaj and Prema, once deeply in love, found their relationship strained as work-related pressures escalated. Long hours at the office became the norm, leaving little time for shared moments. The constant stress and deadlines led to communication breakdowns, turning their home into a silent battleground. Their once vibrant connection eroded under the weight of professional demands, leaving them yearning for the simplicity of the past.

Recognizing the toll work had taken on their relationship, Pankaj and Prema decided to prioritize their connection. They established dedicated "unplugged" time, free from work discussions. Communication improved as they openly shared their feelings and concerns. Together, they set boundaries on work hours and committed to rejuvenating their bond. Seeking support from each other, they navigated the challenges as a team, ultimately rediscovering the strength of their relationship amid life's demands..

Health problems,

, either of one of the partners or a family member, can be a significant stressor. For instance, if one partner has a chronic illness, it can place emotional and financial burdens on the relationship.

Pallavi and Prashant

Pallavi and Prashant faced a daunting challenge after a decade of marital bliss: Prashant was diagnosed with severe kidney issues, threatening their family's stability. Undeterred, Pallavi, driven by love, shouldered the financial burden by dedicating extra hours to her coaching center and engaging in online work.

Meanwhile, Prashant, recognizing the importance of his health, opted for less strenuous projects and focused on spending quality time with their two daughters. Together, they navigated the turbulent waters of health concerns while fortifying their family bonds.

As the years passed, their resilience paid off. Their daughters, now grown and studying abroad, thrived in their pursuits. Pallavi, unwavering in her commitment, not only ensured their financial stability but also pursued her dreams. She traveled the world for work, sometimes with Prashant, sometimes solo, proving that love and determination can conquer even the most challenging obstacles.

In the face of adversity, Pallavi and Prashant not only preserved their relationship but also flourished individually. Today, they stand as proud parents, their journey serving as a testament to the power of love, perseverance, and unwavering support.

as exemplified by Pallavi and Prashant, can pose significant challenges. Prashant's severe kidney issues threatened their family's stability, but Pallavi's unwavering commitment and adaptability helped them navigate the turbulent waters. Together, they emerged resilient, proving that love, perseverance, and unwavering support can conquer even the most challenging obstacles.

Parenting challenges and long-distance relationships add further dimensions to the complexities couples face. Nitya and Naman navigated the hurdles of a long-distance relationship, choosing either to triumph over trials or drift apart. Their story illustrates the impact of commitment and trust in overcoming distance.

Nitya and naman

In a world connected by screens, Nitya and Naman embarked on a challenging long-distance relationship, battling time zones and technological glitches. Despite the miles, their love thrived initially.

Ending 1 - Triumph over Trials:

They faced communication hurdles and misunderstandings, but their commitment prevailed. Late-night video calls, surprise virtual dates, and handwritten letters kept the flame alive. They learned to trust and appreciate each other's independence. The challenges strengthened their bond, and after two years, Nitya and Naman closed the distance, realizing that love can conquer miles.

Ending 2 - Drifting Apart:

Over time, the distance took its toll. Trust issues crept in, and misunderstandings festered. The lack of physical presence led to a growing emotional gap. Despite efforts, their connection weakened. Eventually, Nitya and Naman acknowledged the strain and chose different paths, realizing that sometimes love isn't enough to bridge the miles.

In both endings, Nitya and Naman's journey reflects the complexities of long-distance relationships and how the outcome can be shaped by the resilience or fragility of the love they share.

7. **Cultural or Religious Differences**: If partners come from different cultural or religious backgrounds, conflicts related to traditions, beliefs, or customs can arise and become external stressors.

8**Traumatic Events**: Experiencing a traumatic event, such as a natural disaster, accident, or loss of a loved one, can place significant emotional stress on a relationship as both partners cope with the aftermath.

Prajakta and her shattered life

Prajakta's world shattered when she lost her one-year-old child, plunging her into a deep depression. The weight of grief strained her relationships with family members, pushing them to the brink of collapse. In this challenging time, Manan, her partner, took on the role of a compassionate caregiver.

Manan researched grief counseling, connecting Prajakta with support groups and therapists who specialized in dealing with loss. He became a pillar of strength, offering a listening ear when she needed to express her pain. Recognizing the strain on their relationship, Manan sought couples counseling to navigate the emotional turmoil together.

Understanding the importance of self-care, Manan encouraged Prajakta to engage in activities that brought her solace, whether it was painting, journaling, or taking long walks. He took on more responsibilities at home, ensuring that the burden wasn't solely on Prajakta's shoulders.

Through perseverance and empathy, Manan played a pivotal role in rebuilding the fragile bonds within the family. Slowly, with time and understanding, Prajakta began to find glimpses of healing, and the family started to rediscover a sense of unity. The journey was arduous, but Manan's unwavering support became the catalyst for their collective healing.

9. **Addiction Issues**: Substance abuse or addiction problems by one partner can have a detrimental impact on the relationship, causing trust issues and emotional turmoil.

Minal and Vandu's love story began with passion and promise. However, as Vandu's drinking and gambling habits escalated, their relationship faced turbulence. Minal, torn between love and turmoil, grappled with the decision to salvage the relationship or walk away from the chaos. The emotional toll pushed her to confront Vandu about his destructive behavior, urging him to seek help. Whether Minal's love could conquer Vandu's demons or if she would find strength to break free remained uncertain.

Solution 1:

Despite Minal's heartfelt plea, Vandu struggled to overcome his vices. The toxicity of his habits continued to poison their relationship, leaving Minal emotionally drained. Realizing the importance of her own well-being, Minal made the painful decision to walk away, choosing to rebuild her life without the constant turmoil. It was a difficult farewell, but Minal found solace in prioritizing her own happiness, leaving the door open for personal growth and new beginnings.

Solution 2:

Minal's unwavering support and Vandu's realization of the damage he was causing prompted a change. Vandu sought professional help to overcome his addictions, demonstrating a sincere commitment to their relationship. Through counseling and dedication, Vandu gradually broke free from the destructive cycle. Minal's decision to stand by him during the darkest times bore fruit as they emerged stronger, their love prevailing over adversity. Together, they faced the challenges head-on, creating a narrative of redemption and resilience.

Overcoming addiction often involves a combination of professional help, support from loved ones, and personal determination. Consider seeking therapy, joining support groups, and establishing a healthy routine. It's crucial to address the root causes and develop coping strategies.

In the realm of addiction, Minal and Vandu faced the tumultuous journey of overcoming destructive habits. Minal's tough decision to walk away in one scenario highlights the importance of prioritizing personal well-being, while in the other, Vandu's commitment to change emphasizes the redemptive power of love.

10. **Social Pressures**: External societal expectations, like societal norms about gender roles or relationship milestones, can create stress if they don't align with the couple's values or desires.

It's important for couples to recognize these external stressors and communicate openly about how they are affecting the relationship. Seeking support from a therapist or counselor can be helpful in managing and resolving these issues. Additionally, building resilience and coping strategies as a couple can strengthen the relationship in the face of external stressors.

Nilesh and Nanda, a couple with an unconventional dynamic, found themselves navigating societal expectations. Nanda, a high-ranking professional, shouldered the financial responsibilities, while Nilesh dedicated himself to household chores and the upbringing of their children. Despite the harmony within their family, external pressure began to cast a shadow.

As their children entered school, whispers and snide remarks fueled by societal norms infiltrated their lives. The kids, once oblivious to societal expectations, began to feel the weight of the comments. Schoolmates mocked them, and the societal disapproval of their unique family structure started to impact their self-esteem.

The children, influenced by societal expectations, began resenting Nilesh for deviating from traditional gender roles. The once tight-knit family faced strains as the children distanced themselves from their father. Nilesh, sensing the growing tension, decided it was time for a candid family conversation.

One evening, Nilesh and Nanda gathered their children and, with honesty and vulnerability, shared their journey, choices, and the love that defined their family. They explained that roles within a family could be diverse, and the essence of a loving home wasn't confined by traditional stereotypes. They encouraged their kids to embrace diversity, challenge societal norms, and prioritize authenticity.

Slowly, the children began to understand the strength in their family's unique structure. Nilesh's role as a supportive partner and homemaker became a source of pride rather than embarrassment. The family collectively decided to face societal expectations head-on, promoting understanding and acceptance.

Over the years, the children grew up with open minds, learning to appreciate diverse perspectives and breaking free from societal constraints. Nilesh and Nanda's decision to address the challenges strengthened their bond as a family, fostering resilience and a deep respect for individual choices.

Social pressures, as depicted in Nilesh and Nanda's story, tested their unconventional family dynamic. Confronting societal expectations head-on, they promoted understanding and acceptance within their family.

Lack of effort,

A relationship requires effort from both parties. If one person isn't putting in the work, it can lead to dissatisfaction.

Lack of effort in a relationship can lead to a variety of problems and challenges. Here's an elaboration on this topic:

1. Communication Breakdown: When one or both partners fail to put in effort to communicate effectively, misunderstandings can arise. This breakdown in communication can lead to unresolved conflicts and growing emotional distance.

2. Emotional Disconnect: Effort in a relationship is essential to maintain emotional intimacy. If one partner becomes complacent or neglects their emotional responsibilities, it can result in feelings of neglect, loneliness, and a lack of connection.

Jai, a successful businessman, devoted much of his time to building his empire. His grand gestures, like buying expensive presents and planning exotic trips, were his way of expressing love for Jyoti. Despite the lavish lifestyle, he struggled to connect with her emotionally due to the demanding nature of his work.

One evening, as Jyoti sat alone in their luxurious home, she decided to share her feelings with Jai. "Jai, I appreciate everything you do for us, but I need more than material things. I need you to be present and emotionally available," she confessed.

Caught off guard, Jai responded, "I'm working hard for our future, for us. Can't you see that?"

As time passed, Jai's work pressures intensified. Jyoti, feeling neglected, sought solace in the company of a close friend who provided the emotional support she craved. One day, she found herself confiding in him about the void in her marriage.

Jai, realizing the growing distance, attempted to salvage their relationship. "I know I've been distant, Jyoti. Let's take a break, just the two of us. We can reconnect," he suggested.

But Jyoti, hurt and emotionally drained, replied, "It's too late, Jai. I needed you when I reached out, and you weren't there."

The couple drifted further apart, and Jyoti's emotional connection with her friend deepened. In time, she made the difficult decision to separate from Jai.

Facing the reality of his actions, Jai reflected on the importance of balancing work and personal life. As he stood in their now-empty home, surrounded by remnants of a love he failed to nurture, he realized the true cost of neglecting emotional needs in a relationship.

Quality time,

Spending quality time together is crucial for bonding and maintaining a healthy relationship. A lack of effort can result in partners drifting apart as they prioritize other activities or interests over their time together.

Naveen and Namrata, once inseparable, found their relationship strained as the quality of their time together dwindled. The first signs emerged during their once-cherished Sunday brunches, now replaced by distracted glances at their phones.

One evening, as they sat in their favorite coffee shop, Naveen noticed Namrata scrolling through social media instead of engaging in conversation. Frustrated, he said, "Namrata, we used to enjoy our time together. What happened to those deep conversations we used to have?"

Namrata, eyes still glued to her phone, replied absentmindedly, "Oh, sorry. I was just checking something. Go on, what were you saying?"

Their weekends became a routine of parallel activities rather than shared experiences. Naveen suggested a movie night, hoping to rekindle their connection. As they sat on the couch, Naveen excitedly picked a classic film. However, Namrata, engrossed in work emails, only half-watched. "I just need to finish this," she said, oblivious to Naveen's disappointment.

Gradually, their communication suffered. Conversations turned into monologues, and laughter became scarce. Naveen attempted to address the issue, saying, "Namrata, I miss us. We're physically together, but it feels like we're miles apart. Can we focus on each other when we're spending time together?"

Namrata nodded, promising change, but old habits persisted. Their date nights turned into silent dinners with occasional small talk. Naveen's attempts to share his day were met with half-hearted responses. "I'm tired," Namrata would say, shutting down any chance for meaningful connection.

One day, Naveen confronted Namrata about the growing distance. "Namrata, our relationship is slipping away. We need to prioritize each other and rebuild what we had." Namrata, finally realizing the gravity of the situation, sighed, "I didn't realize it had gotten this bad. I want to change, Naveen, I really do."

They decided to implement "tech-free" hours and rediscover shared hobbies. Gradually, the quality of their time improved, and they began to reconnect. It wasn't easy, but the realization that their relationship needed attention motivated them to rebuild what was almost lost.

In the end, Naveen and Namrata learned that quality time was the lifeline of their relationship, and by making intentional efforts to be present, they salvaged what was on the verge of slipping away..

Neglected needs,

Partners have various emotional, physical, and psychological needs. When effort is lacking, these needs may go unmet, causing frustration and dissatisfaction within the relationship.

Tanu and Tapan had been a couple for several years, their love blooming amid shared dreams and laughter. However, Tapan's demanding job began to cast a shadow over their relationship. He was often burdened with heavy workloads and frequent travel, leaving Tanu feeling neglected and unfulfilled.

One evening, as Tanu waited for Tapan to come home, she couldn't shake the frustration that had been building within her. The promises of quality time together were often overshadowed by work calls and last-minute trips. This emotional void led Tanu to seek solace in the companionship of her fitness instructor, Aarav, who had been a consistent and understanding presence in her life.

As Tanu and Aarav spent more time together, the boundaries of their relationship blurred. One day, Tapan, sensing the growing distance, confronted Tanu about her changed behavior. Tanu, feeling cornered, admitted to her involvement with Aarav, citing her unmet emotional needs as the reason.

Tapan, hurt and surprised, argued that communication would have been a better outlet for her frustrations. Tanu countered, expressing how she had tried talking to him multiple times, only to feel unheard and unimportant. The couple found themselves at an impasse, grappling with the consequences of their choices.

In the end, Tanu and Tapan decided to part ways. Tanu acknowledged that seeking companionship outside the relationship wasn't the solution and regretted not persisting in communicating her needs. Tapan, on the other hand, recognized the toll his work had taken on their relationship and vowed to prioritize his personal life moving forward.

This story highlights the importance of open communication and compromise in relationships, urging individuals to address issues directly rather than seeking fulfillment elsewhere.

But what if partner is not ready to listen and understand

If one partner feels unheard or misunderstood, it's crucial to explore alternative communication methods and perhaps seek external support, such as couples counseling. Relationships require effort from both parties, and finding a neutral third party to facilitate discussions can sometimes break down communication barriers. If, despite sincere attempts, communication remains difficult, individuals may need to evaluate the overall health of the relationship and consider whether it's meeting their emotional needs. It's important to prioritize mental and emotional well-being while making thoughtful decisions about the future of the relationship.

Couple counselling is possible only when both partners are ready to work together on their relationship, in this case Tapan is not interested what should Tanu do

If Tapan is unwilling to engage in couples counseling or work together on the relationship, Tanu might need to prioritize her own well-being. It's essential for her to consider her own needs and whether the relationship is meeting them. In such situations, individual counseling for Tanu could provide a supportive space to navigate her emotions, explore options, and make decisions about her future.

While it's challenging when both partners are not on the same page, Tanu's focus should be on self-care and personal growth. This may involve setting clear boundaries, expressing her needs assertively, and deciding if the relationship aligns with her long-term happiness. Ultimately, individuals deserve to be in relationships where their emotional well-being is considered, and sometimes that means making tough decisions for personal growth and fulfillment.

as seen in Tanu and Tapan's story, reveal how unmet emotional needs can lead to emotional infidelity. Tanu's journey illustrates the complexities of seeking companionship outside the relationship.

In scenarios where one partner feels unheard, seeking external support, such as couples counseling, becomes essential. If a partner is unwilling to engage in counseling, prioritizing personal well-being and considering the overall health of the relationship becomes crucial.

Deterioration of trust and diminished romance underscore the importance of consistent effort in relationships. The impact of diminishing romance is explained by the gradual shift from passionate beginnings to routine-oriented dynamics.

Resentment and frustration, exemplified in Tapan and Tanmay's story, showcase how the toxic cycle of blame and negativity can lead to a breaking point. Reflection and redemption become vital for rebuilding a relationship.

The vulnerability to infidelity in Malti and Shashank's narrative emphasizes the consequences of neglect and undervaluation. The story serves as a cautionary tale, highlighting the importance of understanding and addressing emotional voids in a relationship.

Drifting apart, the ultimate consequence of a consistent lack of effort, leads to reflection and redemption, emphasizing the shared responsibility of effort in a relationship.

Compatibility issues are explored in-depth, covering aspects such as communication styles, values, interests, lifestyle choices, emotional compatibility, sexual compatibility, conflict resolution, long-term goals, and personality traits. The importance of finding common ground and building a strong foundation is emphasized.

Vandana and Abhinav, Pankaj and Prema, Pallavi and Prashant, Nitya and Naman, Prajakta and Manan, Minal and Vandu, Nilesh and Nanda, Jai and Jyoti, Naveen and Namrata, Tanu and Tapan, and Tapan and Tanmay represent diverse couples facing distinct challenges. Their stories weave a comprehensive narrative about the intricacies of relationships and the essential role of effort, communication, and understanding in overcoming obstacles.

Certainly! Here is a proofread version of the provided text:

In both endings, Nitya and Naman's journey reflects the complexities of long-distance relationships and how the outcome can be shaped by the resilience or fragility of the love they share.

7. Cultural or Religious Differences: Partners from different cultural or religious backgrounds may face conflicts related to traditions, beliefs, or customs, becoming external stressors.

Prajakta's world shattered when she lost her one-year-old child, plunging her into a deep depression. The weight of grief strained her relationships with family members, pushing them to the brink of collapse. In this challenging time, Manan, her partner, took on the role of a compassionate caregiver.

Manan researched grief counseling, connecting Prajakta with support groups and therapists specializing in dealing with loss. He became a pillar of strength, offering a listening ear when she needed to express her pain. Recognizing the strain on their relationship, Manan sought couples counseling to navigate the emotional turmoil together.

Understanding the importance of self-care, Manan encouraged Prajakta to engage in activities that brought her solace, whether it was painting, journaling, or taking long walks. He took on more responsibilities at home, ensuring that the burden wasn't solely on Prajakta's shoulders.

Through perseverance and empathy, Manan played a pivotal role in rebuilding the fragile bonds within the family. Slowly, with time and understanding, Prajakta began to find glimpses of healing, and the family started to rediscover a sense of unity. The journey was arduous, but Manan's unwavering support became the catalyst for their collective healing.

9. Addiction Issues: Substance abuse or addiction problems by one partner can have a detrimental impact on the relationship, causing trust issues and emotional turmoil.

Minal and Vandu's love story began with passion and promise. However, as Vandu's drinking and gambling habits escalated, their relationship faced turbulence. Minal, torn between love and turmoil, grappled with the decision to salvage the relationship or walk away from the chaos. The emotional toll pushed her to confront Vandu about his destructive behavior, urging him to seek help. Whether Minal's love could conquer Vandu's demons or if she would find strength to break free remained uncertain.

Solution 1:

Despite Minal's heartfelt plea, Vandu struggled to overcome his vices. The toxicity of his habits continued to poison their relationship, leaving Minal emotionally drained. Realizing the importance of her own well-being, Minal made the painful decision to walk away, choosing to rebuild her life without the constant turmoil. It was a difficult farewell, but Minal found solace in prioritizing her own happiness, leaving the door open for personal growth and new beginnings.

Solution 2:

Minal's unwavering support and Vandu's realization of the damage he was causing prompted a change. Vandu sought professional help to overcome his addictions, demonstrating a sincere commitment to their relationship. Through counseling and dedication, Vandu gradually broke free from the destructive cycle. Minal's decision to stand by him during the darkest times bore fruit as they emerged stronger, their love prevailing over adversity. Together, they faced the challenges head-on, creating a narrative of redemption and resilience.

Overcoming addiction often involves a combination of professional help, support from loved ones, and personal determination. Consider seeking therapy, joining support groups, and establishing a healthy routine. It's crucial to address the root causes and develop coping strategies.

10. Social Pressures: External societal expectations, like societal norms about gender roles or relationship milestones, can create stress if they don't align with the couple's values or desires.

Nilesh and Nanda, a couple with an unconventional dynamic, found themselves navigating societal expectations. Nanda, a high-ranking professional, shouldered the financial responsibilities, while Nilesh dedicated himself to household chores and the upbringing of their children. Despite the harmony within their family, external pressure began to cast a shadow.

As their children entered school, whispers and snide remarks fueled by societal norms infiltrated their lives. The kids, once oblivious to societal expectations, began to feel the weight of the comments. Schoolmates mocked them, and the societal disapproval of their unique family structure started to impact their self-esteem.

The children, influenced by societal expectations, began resenting Nilesh for deviating from traditional gender roles. The once tight-knit family faced strains as the children distanced themselves from their father. Nilesh, sensing the growing tension, decided it was time for a candid family conversation.

One evening, Nilesh and Nanda gathered their children and, with honesty and vulnerability, shared their journey, choices, and the love that defined their family. They explained that roles within a family could be diverse, and the essence of a loving home wasn't confined by traditional stereotypes. They encouraged their kids to embrace diversity, challenge societal norms, and prioritize authenticity.

Slowly, the children began to understand the strength in their family's unique structure. Nilesh's role as a supportive partner and homemaker became a source of pride rather than embarrassment. The family collectively decided to face societal expectations head-on, promoting understanding and acceptance.

Over the years, the children grew up with open minds, learning to appreciate diverse perspectives and breaking free from societal constraints. Nilesh and Nanda's decision to address the challenges strengthened their bond as a family, fostering resilience and a deep respect for individual choices.

6. Lack of Effort: A relationship requires effort from both parties. If one person isn't putting in the work, it can lead to dissatisfaction.

Communication Breakdown: When one or both partners fail to put in effort to communicate effectively, misunderstandings can arise. This breakdown in communication can lead to unresolved conflicts and growing emotional distance.

Emotional Disconnect: Effort in a relationship is essential to maintain emotional intimacy. If one partner becomes complacent or neglects their emotional responsibilities, it can result in feelings of neglect, loneliness, and a lack of connection.

Jai, a successful businessman, devoted much of his time to building his empire. His grand gestures, like buying expensive presents and planning exotic trips, were his way of expressing love for Jyoti. Despite the lavish lifestyle, he struggled to connect with her emotionally due to the demanding nature of his work.

One evening, as Jyoti sat alone in their luxurious home, she decided to share her feelings with Jai. "Jai, I appreciate everything you do for us, but I need more than material things. I need you to be present and emotionally available," she confessed.

Caught off guard, Jai responded, "I'm working hard for our future, for us. Can't you see that?"

As time passed, Jai's work pressures intensified. Jyoti, feeling neglected, sought solace in the company of a close friend who provided the emotional support she craved. One day, she found herself confiding in him about the void in her marriage.

Jai, realizing the growing distance, attempted to salvage their relationship. "I know I've been distant, Jyoti. Let's take a break, just the two of us. We can reconnect," he suggested.

But Jyoti, hurt and emotionally drained, replied, "It's too late, Jai. I needed you when I reached out, and you weren't there."

The couple drifted further apart, and Jyoti's emotional connection with her friend deepened. In time, she made

the difficult decision to separate from Jai.

Facing the reality of his actions, Jai reflected on the importance of balancing work and personal life. As he stood in their now-empty home, surrounded by remnants of a love he failed to nurture, he realized the true cost of neglecting emotional needs in a relationship.

Reduced Quality Time: Spending quality time together is crucial for bonding and maintaining a healthy relationship. A lack of effort can result in partners drifting apart as they prioritize other activities or interests over their time together.

Naveen and Namrata, once inseparable, found their relationship strained as the quality of their time together dwindled. The first signs emerged during their once-cherished Sunday brunches, now replaced by distracted glances at their phones.

One evening, as they sat in their favorite coffee shop, Naveen noticed Namrata scrolling through social media instead of engaging in conversation. Frustrated, he said, "Namrata, we used to enjoy our time together. What happened to those deep conversations we used to have?"

Namrata, eyes still glued to her phone, replied absentmindedly, "Oh, sorry. I was just checking something. Go on, what were you saying?"

Their weekends became a routine of parallel activities rather than shared experiences. Naveen suggested a movie night, hoping to rekindle their connection. As they sat on the couch, Naveen excitedly picked a classic film. However, Namrata, engrossed in work emails, only half-watched. "I just need to finish this," she said, oblivious to Naveen's disappointment.

Gradually, their communication suffered. Conversations turned into monologues, and laughter became scarce. Naveen attempted to address the issue, saying, "Namrata, I miss

us. We're physically together, but it feels like we're miles apart. Can we focus on each other when we're spending time together?"

Namrata nodded, promising change, but old habits persisted. Their date nights turned into silent dinners with occasional small talk. Naveen's attempts to share his day were met with half-hearted responses. "I'm tired," Namrata would say, shutting down any chance for meaningful connection.

One day, Naveen confronted Namrata about the growing distance. "Namrata, our relationship is slipping away. We need to prioritize each other and rebuild what we had." Namrata, finally realizing the gravity of the situation, sighed, "I didn't realize it had gotten this bad. I want to change, Naveen, I really do."

They decided to implement "tech-free" hours and rediscover shared hobbies. Gradually, the quality of their time improved, and they began to reconnect. It wasn't easy, but the realization that their relationship needed attention motivated them to rebuild what was almost lost.

In the end, Naveen and Namrata learned that quality time was the lifeline of their relationship, and by making intentional efforts to be present, they salvaged what was on the verge of slipping away.

Neglected Needs: Partners have various emotional, physical, and psychological needs. When effort is lacking, these needs may go unmet, causing frustration and dissatisfaction within the relationship.

Tanu and Tapan had been a couple for several years, their love blooming amid shared dreams and laughter. However, Tapan's demanding job began to cast a shadow over their relationship. He was often burdened with heavy workloads and frequent travel, leaving Tanu feeling neglected and unfulfilled.

One evening, as Tanu waited for Tapan to come home, she couldn't shake the frustration that had been building within her. The promises of quality time together were often overshadowed by work calls and last-minute trips. This emotional void led Tanu to seek solace in the companionship of her fitness instructor, Aarav, who had been a consistent and understanding presence in her life.

As Tanu and Aarav spent more time together, the boundaries of their relationship blurred. One day, Tapan, sensing the growing distance, confronted Tanu about her changed behavior. Tanu, feeling cornered, admitted to her involvement with Aarav, citing her unmet emotional needs as the reason.

Tapan, hurt and surprised, argued that communication would have been a better outlet for her frustrations. Tanu countered, expressing how she had tried talking to him multiple times, only to feel unheard and unimportant. The couple found themselves at an impasse, grappling with the consequences of their choices.

In the end, Tanu and Tapan decided to part ways. Tanu acknowledged that seeking companionship outside the relationship wasn't the solution and regretted not persisting in communicating her needs. Tapan, on the other hand, recognized the toll his work had taken on their relationship and vowed to prioritize his personal life moving forward.

This story highlights the importance of open communication and compromise in relationships, urging individuals to address issues directly rather than seeking fulfillment elsewhere.

But what if the partner is not ready to listen and understand?

If one partner feels unheard or misunderstood, it's crucial to explore alternative communication methods and perhaps seek external support, such as couples counseling. Relationships require effort from both parties, and finding a neutral third party to facilitate discussions can sometimes break down communication barriers. If, despite sincere attempts, communication remains difficult, individuals may need to evaluate the overall health of the relationship and consider whether it's meeting their emotional needs. It's important to prioritize mental and emotional well-being while making thoughtful decisions about the future of the relationship.

Couple counseling is possible only when both partners are ready to work together on their relationship; in this case, Tapan is not interested, what should Tanu do?

If Tapan is unwilling to engage in couples counseling or work together on the relationship, Tanu might need to prioritize her own well-being. It's essential for her to consider her own needs and whether the relationship is meeting them. In such situations, individual counseling for Tanu could provide a supportive space to navigate her emotions, explore options, and make decisions about her future.

While it's challenging when both partners are not on the same page, Tanu's focus should be on self-care and personal growth. This may involve setting clear boundaries, expressing her needs assertively, and deciding if the relationship aligns with her long-term happiness. Ultimately, individuals deserve to be in relationships where their emotional well-being is considered, and sometimes that means making tough decisions for personal growth and fulfillment.

5. Deterioration of Trust: Trust is the foundation of a strong relationship. If one partner consistently fails to follow through on promises or commitments, trust can erode, leading to insecurity and doubt.

6. Diminished Romance: Romance and affection often require effort to keep the spark alive. Neglecting romantic gestures, date nights, or physical intimacy can lead to a decrease in overall satisfaction and passion.

Why romance diminishes

Romance often diminishes over time in relationships due to various factors. Initially, the novelty and excitement of a new connection can create intense romantic feelings. However, as the relationship progresses, familiarity sets in, and partners become more accustomed to each other. This can lead to a shift from the passionate, romantic phase to a more comfortable, routine-oriented dynamic.

Additionally, daily stressors, responsibilities, and external pressures can take a toll on the emotional energy invested in romantic gestures. Couples may prioritize practical aspects of life, inadvertently neglecting the emotional and romantic aspects.

The impact of diminishing romance can be significant, affecting the overall satisfaction and longevity of the relationship. Without ongoing effort to maintain emotional connection and intimacy, partners may feel unfulfilled or disconnected. It's crucial for couples to communicate openly, prioritize quality time, and find ways to reignite the romantic spark to sustain a healthy, long-lasting relationship.

Resentment and Frustration: Over time, one partner's lack of effort can breed resentment and frustration in the other. This can create a toxic cycle of negativity within the relationship.

Scene 1: Tapan and Tanmay's Early Days

Tapan and Tanmay met during their college years. They shared a beautiful connection, filled with laughter and shared dreams. However, Tapan started neglecting his responsibilities, missing dates, and forgetting important occasions.

Tapan: "I'm just busy with work, Tanmay. I'll make it up to you, I promise."

Scene 2: Tanmay's Growing Frustration

As Tapan's lack of effort continued, Tanmay became frustrated.

Tanmay: "I need you to be present in this relationship, Tapan. It's not just about promises; actions matter too."

Scene 3: Arguments and Defensiveness

The couple started having heated arguments.

Tapan: "You're overreacting! I have my own priorities."

Tanmay: "I can't keep being the only one trying, Tapan. It's exhausting."

Scene 4: Resentment Sets In

Resentment began to poison their once-loving relationship.

Tapan: "You're never satisfied. Nothing I do is ever enough for you."

Tanmay: "I just want us to be a team, Tapan. Is that too much to ask?"

Scene 5: The Toxic Cycle

Their relationship turned toxic, marked by blame and negativity.

Tapan: "You're always criticizing me. I can't take it anymore."

Tanmay: "I wouldn't need to if you showed some effort. It's toxic for both of us."

Scene 6: Breaking Point

The toxicity reached its peak, pushing them to a breaking point.

Tapan: "Maybe we're better off apart. I can't live like this."

Tanmay: "If you can't see how your lack of effort affects us, maybe you're right."

Scene 7: Reflection and Redemption

After some time apart, Tapan reflected on his actions and realized the damage he had done.

Tapan: "I was wrong, Tanmay. I took you for granted. I want to make things right."

Tanmay: "Actions speak louder than words, Tapan. Are you willing to change?"

The story emphasizes the impact of neglect and lack of effort on a relationship, leading to a toxic cycle that can be difficult to break.

8. Vulnerability to Infidelity: When partners feel neglected or undervalued due to a lack of effort, they may become more vulnerable to seeking emotional or physical intimacy outside of the relationship, potentially leading to infidelity.

Malti, a woman with dreams as vibrant as the sunrise, found herself in a marriage that resembled a fading sunset. Shashank, her husband, unintentionally became a maestro in the art of neglect, a composer of undervaluation. Each day, Malti's spirit withered like a neglected garden.

As Shashank immersed himself in his career, Malti sought solace in the corners of her own existence. Time passed, and subtle loneliness engulfed her. One day, the warmth of Madhur's friendship beckoned, and Malti found herself drawn to it like a moth to a flame. In the shadows of emotional starvation, Madhur became the unexpected source of nourishment.

Their connection grew, each stolen moment a salve for Malti's neglected heart. Society, always quick to cast judgment, wagged its moralistic finger. Shashank, oblivious to his own role in this unfolding tragedy, pointed accusatory fingers at Malti, blaming her for the fractures in their relationship.

Yet, Malti understood the silent screams of her neglected heart. She knew her actions were a manifestation of the emotional void Shashank had inadvertently created. The affair wasn't a betrayal but a desperate attempt to fill the gaping holes in her heart.

As whispers of infidelity echoed through the corridors of family and society, Malti stood at the crossroads of understanding and judgment. Shashank, finally awakening to the gravity of his neglect, tried to salvage the wreckage of their marriage, but time had become an unsympathetic witness.

Malti, now empowered by self-awareness, faced the consequences with stoic grace. The unraveling of their relationship became a cautionary tale, a reminder that neglect and undervaluation could birth storms capable of tearing even the sturdiest of bonds asunder. In the end, Shashank, burdened by the weight of belated realization, could only watch as the woman he had neglected found her strength elsewhere.--

9. Drifting Apart: Ultimately, a consistent lack of effort can cause partners to drift apart emotionally and, in some cases, lead to the end of the relationship.

It's important to recognize that effort in a relationship should be a shared responsibility, and addressing these issues often involves open and honest communication, reevaluating priorities, and working together to reignite the connection and commitment to the relationship.

Compatibility Issues: Sometimes, people simply aren't well-suited for each other, and their differences cause problems.

Compatibility issues in relationships can manifest in various ways and can lead to significant relationship problems. Here are some elaborations on compatibility issues:

1. Communication Styles: Differences in how individuals communicate can create conflicts. For instance, one person might prefer open and direct communication, while the other might be more reserved or passive-aggressive. These contrasting styles can lead to misunderstandings and frustration.

2. Values and Beliefs: Fundamental differences in values, religious beliefs, or ethical principles can be a substantial source of compatibility problems. If two people have conflicting core values, it can be challenging to find common ground and build a strong, lasting relationship.

3. Interests and Hobbies: When partners have vastly different interests and hobbies, it can be challenging to find activities

they both enjoy. Spending time apart pursuing separate interests can lead to emotional distance in the relationship.

4. Lifestyle Choices: Differences in lifestyle preferences, such as whether to have children, where to live, or how to manage finances, can cause compatibility issues. These disparities can create ongoing tension if not addressed and compromised upon.

5. Emotional Compatibility: Emotional compatibility relates to how individuals handle and express emotions. Some people may be more emotionally expressive, while others are more reserved. A disconnect in emotional styles can lead to feelings of being misunderstood or unsupported.

6. Sexual Compatibility: Differences in sexual desires and preferences can lead to dissatisfaction and frustration in a relationship. It's essential for partners to communicate openly about their needs and desires to work towards a satisfying sexual connection.

7. Conflict Resolution: Discrepancies in how individuals handle conflicts can lead to recurring arguments and unresolved issues. One partner may prefer to address problems immediately, while the other might need time to cool off before discussing things, creating a mismatch in conflict resolution styles.

8. Long-Term Goals: If partners have different long-term goals and aspirations, such as career ambitions or dreams of travel, it can create tension. Finding a balance between individual goals and shared aspirations is crucial for compatibility.

9. Family and Friendships: Conflicts can arise when partners have differing expectations regarding the role of family and friends in their lives. Some may value spending a lot of time

with extended family, while others may prioritize their partner over social relationships.

10. Personality Traits: Compatibility can be affected by differences in personality traits, such as introversion vs. extroversion, spontaneity vs. structure, and optimism vs. pessimism. These differences can influence how individuals approach life and interact with each other.

Addressing compatibility issues in a relationship often requires open and honest communication, compromise, and a willingness to work together to find solutions that accommodate both partners' needs and preferences. In some cases, couples may seek the assistance of a relationship counselor or therapist to navigate these challenges effectively.

It's important to remember that relationships can also be incredibly rewarding and fulfilling when both partners work together to overcome challenges and grow together. If you're experiencing difficulties in a relationship, open and honest communication is often the first step toward resolving issues.

Romantic Relationships

Romantic relationships are diverse and can take many forms, each with its own dynamics and characteristics. Here are some common types of romantic relationships:

1. **Monogamous Relationship**: This is the most traditional form of a romantic relationship, where two individuals exclusively commit to each other. They focus on building a deep emotional connection and often aspire to create a long-term partnership.

2. **Open Relationship**: In an open relationship, partners agree that they can have romantic or sexual interactions with others outside the primary partnership. Communication and

clear boundaries are crucial to making this type of relationship work.

In their open relationship, Naman and Nidhi faced challenges related to communication. Naman assumed Nidhi was comfortable with a certain level of intimacy with others, while Nidhi felt that Naman wasn't keeping her informed about his interactions. This lack of clear communication led to misunderstandings, causing tension between them. Establishing and regularly revisiting boundaries and expectations could have helped them navigate these issues more smoothly.

3. **Polyamorous Relationship**: Polyamory involves engaging in multiple romantic or sexual relationships simultaneously, with the knowledge and consent of all involved parties. Trust, honesty, and effective communication are essential in polyamorous relationships.

4. **Long-Distance Relationship**: When partners live far apart, they maintain their romantic connection through communication and occasional visits. Trust and effective communication are vital in making long-distance relationships function.

5. **Casual Dating**: Some people prefer to keep things light and non-committal, engaging in casual dating where they enjoy each other's company without the expectation of a serious relationship. These relationships can be short-term or evolve into something more.

6. **Same-Sex Relationship**: These are romantic relationships between individuals of the same gender. They function similarly to heterosexual relationships but may face unique challenges related to societal acceptance and legal recognition.

7. **Age-Gap Relationship**: Partners in these relationships have a significant difference in age. Managing generational gaps and expectations can be a key factor in making these relationships work.

8. **Interracial or Interethnic Relationship**: These relationships involve individuals from different racial or ethnic backgrounds. Cultural understanding, respect, and communication are crucial to navigate potential cultural differences.

9. **Arranged Marriage**: In some cultures, marriages are arranged by families, and the couple may not know each other well before marriage. These relationships rely on mutual respect and a willingness to adapt and grow together.

10. **LGBTQ+ Relationships**: These encompass a range of relationships among LGBTQ+ individuals. While they function similarly to heterosexual relationships, they may involve additional challenges related to discrimination and social acceptance.

In all types of romantic relationships, communication, trust, and mutual respect are foundational. The specific dynamics and functions of a relationship depend on the individuals involved, their goals, and their unique circumstances. Successful romantic relationships often require effort, compromise, and a willingness to grow and adapt together.

Why isn't an open relationship accepted by society?

Societal acceptance of open relationships varies greatly across cultures, communities, and individuals. It's important to recognize that attitudes toward open relationships are not universally negative, and opinions on this matter can be highly subjective. However, there are several reasons why some people or societies may be less accepting of open relationships:

1. **Traditional Values**: Many societies have deeply ingrained traditional values that prioritize monogamy as the ideal form of a romantic relationship. These values can be influenced by religious beliefs, cultural norms, and historical practices.

2. **Jealousy and Insecurity**: Open relationships often challenge the notions of exclusivity and can trigger feelings of jealousy and insecurity in some individuals. This discomfort can lead to negative perceptions of open relationships.

3. **Fear of Relationship Instability**: Some people believe that open relationships are less stable and more likely to lead to emotional turmoil or a breakup. The idea of having multiple partners can be seen as a potential source of instability.

4. **Lack of Understanding**: Open relationships can be misunderstood or misrepresented in media and popular culture. This lack of understanding can contribute to negative stereotypes and misconceptions.

5. **Social Stigma**: Open relationships can face social stigma and discrimination. People in open relationships may fear judgment or discrimination from family, friends, or colleagues, which can discourage them from being open about their relationship choices.

6. **Legal and Financial Complexities**: In some places, legal and financial structures are primarily designed for monogamous couples, which can create challenges for those in open relationships when it comes to issues like inheritance, healthcare, or child custody.

7. **Moral or Religious Beliefs**: Some individuals or communities have strong moral or religious objections to non-

monogamous relationships, considering them sinful or immoral.

It's important to note that these reasons for societal non-acceptance are not universal, and attitudes toward open relationships are evolving in many places. Open relationships are a valid choice for consenting adults who communicate openly and honestly about their desires and boundaries. Ultimately, societal acceptance or rejection of open relationships is a complex and culturally specific issue that continues to evolve over time.

~

Polyamorous relationships can function well when all parties involved communicate openly, honestly, and consent to the arrangement. In polyamory, individuals have multiple romantic or sexual relationships with the knowledge and consent of all parties. Here's how they typically function and some factors that can contribute to happiness and contentment:

1. **Communication**: Effective communication is paramount in polyamorous relationships. All partners must discuss their needs, boundaries, and expectations regularly. Honest and clear communication helps build trust and maintain a healthy balance among multiple relationships.

2. **Consent**: Everyone involved in a polyamorous relationship should willingly and enthusiastically consent to the arrangement. Consent ensures that all parties are comfortable with the dynamics and can make informed decisions.

3. **Boundaries**: Establishing and respecting boundaries is crucial. Partners in polyamorous relationships should have a clear understanding of what is acceptable behavior within the

relationship and what is not. Boundaries help prevent misunderstandings and conflicts.

4. **Emotional Management**: Managing emotions can be more complex in polyamorous relationships due to multiple connections. Partners must be emotionally mature and supportive, handling jealousy, insecurity, and other feelings in a healthy manner.

5. **Time Management**: Balancing time among multiple partners can be challenging. Successful polyamorous relationships require good time management and prioritization to ensure that each partner feels valued and appreciated.

6. **Trust and Honesty**: Trust is the foundation of any relationship, and it's even more critical in polyamory. Being honest about feelings, desires, and other relationships is essential to maintain trust.

7. **Compersion**: Compersion is the positive feeling one experiences when witnessing their partner's happiness with someone else. Cultivating compersion rather than jealousy can lead to greater happiness in polyamorous relationships.

8. **Community and Support**: Some people find it helpful to connect with like-minded individuals in the polyamorous community for advice, support, and understanding.

As for happiness and contentment, polyamorous relationships can indeed lead to fulfillment for those who choose this lifestyle. Many people in polyamorous relationships report feeling a deeper sense of personal growth, expanded emotional connections, and enhanced communication skills. However, it's important to note that polyamory is not suitable for everyone, and not all individuals or couples may find happiness in this type of arrangement.

The key is to be self-aware, communicate openly, and prioritize the well-being of all involved. Some individuals and couples are very content and fulfilled in polyamorous relationships, while others may prefer monogamy. Ultimately, the success and happiness in any type of relationship depend on the compatibility, values, and communication skills of the individuals involved.--

Is casual dating perfect for healthy romantic relationships?

Casual dating can be a valid and enjoyable way to engage in romantic relationships, but whether it's "perfect" for healthy romantic relationships depends on individual preferences, goals, and circumstances. Here are some considerations:

Pros of Casual Dating for Healthy Relationships:

1. **Low Pressure**: Casual dating allows individuals to enjoy the company of others without the immediate pressure of long-term commitment. It can be a low-stress way to get to know different people.

2. **Exploration**: It provides an opportunity to explore different personalities and dating experiences, helping individuals gain a better understanding of their own preferences and needs in a partner.

3. **Independence**: Casual dating often allows for greater personal independence and freedom, as there are typically fewer expectations and obligations compared to more serious relationships.

4. **Focus on Self-Growth**: It can be a time for self-discovery and self-growth, as individuals have the freedom to prioritize personal development and pursue their own interests.

5. **Flexibility**: Casual dating can be adaptable to changing life circumstances, making it suitable for people who have busy or uncertain schedules.

Cons of Casual Dating for Healthy Relationships:

1. **Emotional Complexity**: Casual dating can become emotionally complex, as feelings may develop over time, leading to confusion or heartache if both partners are not on the same page.

2. **Lack of Commitment**: Some individuals may find that casual dating lacks the emotional depth and security they desire in a long-term relationship.

3. **Misaligned Expectations**: If one person is looking for a committed relationship while the other is only interested in casual dating, it can lead to disappointment and conflict.

4. **Risk of Miscommunication**: Clear communication is essential in casual dating to avoid misunderstandings or unintentional hurt feelings.

5. **Social Stigma**: In some cultures or communities, casual dating may be stigmatized or not well-accepted.

Whether casual dating is perfect for a healthy romantic relationship depends on the individuals involved and their mutual understanding. It can be a great fit for those who prioritize personal freedom and exploration or for individuals who are not ready for a committed relationship at a particular stage in their lives.

However, it's essential that all parties involved are on the same page regarding their expectations and intentions to ensure that the casual dating experience remains positive and respectful. Open and honest communication is key to navigating the complexities of casual dating and maintaining healthy relationships, whether they are casual or long-term commitments.

How are heterosexual and same-sex relationships similar? How can romance be missing in a heterosexual relationship but not in a same-sex relationship?

Heterosexual and same-sex relationships share many similarities, as both involve romantic and emotional connections between individuals. Love, affection, and the desire for emotional intimacy are universal aspects of human relationships that can be present in both heterosexual and same-sex couples. However, there are also unique experiences and challenges associated with each type of relationship.

Common Elements in Both Heterosexual and Same-Sex Relationships:

1. **Emotional Connection**: Both types of relationships can involve a deep emotional connection where partners care for and support each other.

2. **Romantic Love**: Romantic feelings, attraction, and love can be present in both heterosexual and same-sex couples.

3. **Intimacy**: Emotional and physical intimacy are important in both types of relationships, contributing to the sense of closeness and connection.

4. **Commitment**: Many heterosexual and same-sex couples commit to long-term partnerships, which can involve shared goals, living arrangements, and responsibilities.

5. **Challenges**: Both types of relationships can face challenges such as communication issues, conflicts, and external pressures.

Differences in the Experience of Romance:

The idea that romance may be missing in a heterosexual relationship but not in a same-sex relationship is a subjective notion that varies greatly among individuals and couples. It's important to avoid making sweeping generalizations, as the presence or absence of romance is not determined by sexual orientation but rather by individual personalities, preferences, and relationship dynamics. Some key points to consider:

1. **Individual Differences**: The presence or absence of romance is highly individual. Some heterosexual couples may have intensely romantic relationships, while others may not prioritize or express romance in the same way.

2. **Relationship Dynamics**: Romance can manifest differently in various relationships. Some couples express their love through romantic gestures, while others emphasize other forms of connection, such as shared interests, humor, or emotional support.

3. **External Factors**: External factors, such as stress, work-life balance, or health issues, can affect the perception of romance in any relationship, regardless of sexual orientation.

4. **Cultural and Societal Influences**: Cultural and societal norms can influence how people express and perceive romance, but these norms can vary widely between cultures and change over time.

Ultimately, the presence or absence of romance in a relationship is a complex and personal matter that depends on the individuals involved, their unique dynamics, and their preferences. It's essential to avoid making assumptions about the nature of any relationship based solely on sexual orientation, as love and connection can be found in all types of partnerships.

How successful are age-gap romantic relationships?

The success of an age-gap romantic relationship depends on various factors, and there is no one-size-fits-all answer. Age-gap relationships can be successful and fulfilling for many couples, but they also come with unique challenges that need to be navigated effectively. Here are some factors to consider:

1. Communication: Effective communication is crucial in any relationship, but it becomes even more essential in age-gap relationships. Open and honest discussions about expectations, life goals, and concerns are key to building a strong foundation.

2. Shared Values and Goals: Partners should share common values and have compatible life goals, or they should be willing to compromise and find ways to harmonize their aspirations despite the age difference.

3. Emotional Connection: A strong emotional connection is essential for relationship success. Both partners should feel loved, respected, and emotionally fulfilled in the relationship.

4. Respect and Equality: Age-gap relationships should be built on mutual respect and equality. Neither partner should feel inferior or superior due to age.

5. Supportive Social Circles: The support of friends and family can significantly impact the success of an age-gap relationship. Acceptance and understanding from loved ones can make it easier to overcome challenges.

6. Handling Life Stages: Partners may be at different life stages due to the age difference. It's important to discuss and plan for how to handle issues like retirement, family planning, and career changes.

7. Coping with Age-Related Differences: Age-gap couples may face challenges related to differences in energy levels, interests, and health. Open discussions and adaptability are key to addressing these issues.

8. Legal and Financial Considerations: Be aware of legal and financial implications, such as inheritance, retirement, and healthcare, that can be affected by the age gap.

It's worth noting that many age-gap relationships are successful and happy. Age differences, while significant, do not necessarily determine the quality or longevity of a relationship. Compatibility, emotional connection, and a willingness to work through challenges are far more critical factors.

Ultimately, the success of an age-gap relationship depends on the individuals involved and how well they communicate, understand, and support each other. If both partners are committed to making the relationship work and are willing to address any issues that arise due to the age gap, there's a good chance of building a healthy and fulfilling partnership.

Why do friendships break?

Friendships can break for various reasons, just like any other relationship. Some common reasons include:

1. **Conflict:** Disagreements or conflicts, if not resolved, can strain or break a friendship.

Conflicts In Friendship

Once upon a time in a quiet suburban neighborhood, there lived two inseparable friends, Sarah and Emily. They had been best friends since their kindergarten days, sharing secrets, dreams, and countless adventures. Their bond was unbreakable, or so they thought.

As they entered their teenage years, the winds of change began to blow through their friendship. Sarah had always been the more outgoing and adventurous of the two, while Emily was quieter and preferred spending time reading and painting. These differences had never been an issue before, but as they matured, their contrasting interests started to create rifts.

One fateful summer, Sarah proposed a road trip with their other friends, a journey filled with thrill and excitement. Emily, however, had different plans. She had been selected to attend a prestigious art camp, which would help her hone her talents. Emily believed this was a golden opportunity to pursue her passion, while Sarah saw it as a betrayal of their friendship.

Tensions began to simmer beneath the surface. Emily felt Sarah didn't understand her dreams, and Sarah felt abandoned and unimportant. They started arguing more frequently, and their once-harmonious friendship was replaced by bitterness and resentment.

One evening, during a heated argument, hurtful words were exchanged. Emily accused Sarah of being selfish and not supporting her dreams, while Sarah accused Emily of prioritizing art over their friendship. The argument escalated, and they parted ways that night, not realizing it would be the last time they spoke for a long while.

Months turned into years, and their friendship remained in tatters. Sarah went on her road trip, while Emily attended the art camp and later pursued a successful career in the art world. Both achieved their dreams, but at the cost of their once-unbreakable friendship.

Years later, a chance encounter brought them face to face. They were older, wiser, and had experienced the highs and lows of life. Seeing each other reignited the memories of their shared childhood adventures and laughter. They realized the pettiness of their conflict in their teenage years and how much they had missed each other.

With tears in their eyes, they apologized and embraced. They understood that their differences didn't have to tear them apart; instead, they could celebrate and support each other's unique paths. Their friendship was rekindled, stronger than ever, but they both knew that it had taken the painful experience of conflict to truly appreciate and cherish what they had together.

In the end, their friendship had weathered the storms of conflict and emerged stronger, a testament to the enduring power of true friendship and the importance of understanding, forgiveness, and growth.

2. **Change:** People change over time, and sometimes friends grow apart due to different life paths, interests, or values.

Changes

Once upon a time in a quiet, picturesque village, there lived two inseparable friends named Sarah and Emma. Their friendship was like a beautiful garden, full of vibrant flowers that had bloomed over many years of shared laughter, secrets, and adventures.

Sarah and Emma had always been peas in a pod, but as they grew older, changes began to creep into their lives. Emma got a job in the bustling city nearby, while Sarah stayed in the serene village, content with her peaceful life. The differences in their lifestyles slowly started to create distance between them.

Emma's hectic city life left her with limited time to visit the village and spend time with Sarah. Sarah, on the other hand, couldn't relate to Emma's fast-paced world and the stress that came with it. Their conversations shifted from heartwarming talks about their dreams to brief, superficial exchanges about work and the weather.

One day, Emma received a promotion that required even more of her time and energy. She had to relocate to a different city, further widening the gap between her and Sarah. Their calls became less frequent, and the visits almost non-existent.

As time passed, Sarah felt left behind, and Emma felt isolated from her old friend. Their once-beautiful friendship had withered, like a neglected garden. They had both changed, and those changes had become insurmountable walls between them.

One evening, Sarah and Emma met by chance in the village park. Awkward smiles were exchanged, but the connection they once had was nowhere to be found. They exchanged polite pleasantries, but it was clear that the bond they once cherished had faded away.

With heavy hearts, they parted ways, each going in a different direction. Their beautiful friendship, once vibrant and full of life, had come to an end, not because they wanted it to, but because the changes in their lives had grown too vast to bridge.

And so, in that quiet village, the garden of their friendship, once in full bloom, lay forgotten, a poignant reminder that sometimes, no matter how beautiful a friendship may have been, changes can bring it to an unexpected and bittersweet end.

3. **Lack of Communication:** If communication dwindles, it can lead to misunderstandings and distance.

Communication

Once upon a time in a peaceful little town, there were two inseparable friends named Nishi and Sudha. They had been friends since childhood, and their bond was as beautiful as the sunsets that painted the sky in hues of orange and pink.

Nishi was a talented artist, while Sudha had a green thumb and could make any garden flourish. Together, they had created countless memories and cherished moments. They laughed together, cried together, and supported each other through thick and thin.

But as the years passed, life's responsibilities began to take hold of them. Nishi's art career was demanding, requiring her to travel often, while Sudha had a growing family to care for. Their once-daily conversations became weekly, then monthly, and eventually, they barely spoke at all.

Misunderstandings crept in like weeds in a neglected garden. Nishi felt neglected and thought Sudha had no time for her anymore, while Sudha assumed Nishi had moved on and made new, more exciting friends. The truth was, neither of them wanted to admit how much they missed each other.

One fateful day, Nishi received a wedding invitation from Sudha. It was a surprise, as they hadn't talked for months. Nishi assumed it was a token invite, a mere formality. She decided not to attend, thinking Sudha wouldn't notice or care. In reality, Sudha had sent the invitation with the hope of rekindling their friendship, not realizing how hurt Nishi felt.

The wedding day came and went, and Sudha noticed Nishi's absence. Hurt by this, she felt that Nishi had abandoned her during one of the most significant moments of her life. Sudha's disappointment turned into resentment, and she stopped reaching out to Nishi altogether.

Months turned into years, and their once-beautiful friendship withered away like a forgotten flower in the garden. Both Nishi and Sudha missed each other terribly but were too stubborn and hurt to take the first step towards reconciliation. The lack of communication, fueled by misunderstandings and unexpressed feelings, had torn apart their once unbreakable bond.

It was only when they stumbled upon an old photograph of themselves as carefree children that they realized how much they had lost. Regret flooded their hearts, and they finally mustered the courage to reach out to each other. Tears were shed, apologies were made, and slowly but surely, they started to rebuild what was once a beautiful friendship.

They learned that communication is the lifeline of any relationship, and assumptions and misunderstandings can be the poison that destroys it. Through open and honest conversations, they nurtured their friendship back to life, like tending to a garden that had been neglected for far too long.

In the end, Nishi and Sudha discovered that a beautiful friendship, once fractured by the lack of communication, could be mended with love, understanding, and the willingness to reconnect. They vowed never to let their bond weaken again, knowing that true friendships, like the most delicate of flowers, require constant care and nurturing to thrive.

4. **Betrayal or Trust Issues:** Trust is vital in friendships, and betrayals or breaches of trust can lead to the end of a friendship.

Betrayal

Shattered Loyalties

Once upon a time in a small, tight-knit town, there lived two inseparable friends, Saral and Mannat. They had been through everything together since childhood, sharing secrets, dreams, and even their darkest fears. Their bond was the envy of the entire community.

One summer, as the town's annual fair approached, Saral and Mannat decided to enter a baking competition. They spent weeks perfecting their recipes and practicing their techniques. As the big day arrived, they were confident that their friendship would make them unbeatable.

However, that morning, a mysterious incident occurred. Saral's secret recipe for her famous blueberry pie disappeared from her kitchen. She searched high and low but couldn't find it anywhere. With the competition only hours away, panic set in.

Mannat, who had always been known for her honesty, offered to help. She said she had an old family recipe that was sure to win. Saral hesitated but agreed, trusting her friend implicitly. They baked Mannat's recipe, a raspberry tart, and headed to the fair.

To their surprise, they didn't win. In fact, they didn't even place. It was a shock, as both of them were talented bakers. Saral couldn't shake the feeling that something was amiss. That night, she decided to confront Mannat.

Tears welled up in Mannat's eyes as she confessed. She had taken Saral's blueberry pie recipe because she thought it was better than her own. She had never intended to hurt Saral, only to win. She deeply regretted her betrayal.

Saral felt her heart shatter as she realized the depth of Mannat's betrayal. Trust, which had been the foundation of their friendship, had crumbled. Their bond was irrevocably damaged, and they went their separate ways.

Years passed, and the memory of their broken friendship haunted them both. Saral learned to forgive, but trust didn't come as easily. Mannat carried the guilt of her actions, vowing never to betray another friend again.

The story of Saral and Mannat serves as a reminder that trust is fragile and can be shattered in an instant, even among the closest of friends. It also teaches us the importance of forgiveness and the possibility of rebuilding trust, although scars may always remain.

5. Life Transitions: Major life events, such as moving, marriage, or starting a family, can affect the time and energy available for friendships.

Life transition

Once upon a time in a quiet suburban neighborhood, there lived two inseparable friends, Sarah and Emman. They had been best friends since their kindergarten days, sharing secrets, dreams, and countless adventures. Their bond was unbreakable, or so they thought.

As the years passed, life brought about significant changes. Sarah's family moved to a bustling city, while Emman's remained in their familiar suburban home. Despite the distance, they vowed to maintain their friendship, promising to write letters and visit during school breaks.

The first few months were filled with heartfelt letters and excited plans for Emman to visit Sarah in the city. But soon, the busyness of high school and new friendships took over, and their letters grew infrequent. Emman made her own friends in the suburban neighborhood, and Sarah found her place in the city's vibrant social scene.

Years passed, and their visits became sporadic at best. Sarah's urban life was a whirlwind of excitement, while Emman found solace in the simplicity of her suburban existence. The two friends had grown apart, no longer sharing the same interests, dreams, or even the same language of friendship they once had.

One summer, Emman decided to visit Sarah, hoping to rekindle their friendship. She was greeted by a Sarah who seemed like a stranger – surrounded by a different group of friends, immersed in a world of urban culture that Emman couldn't relate to. Their time together felt awkward, and the silence between them grew deafening.

Emman returned home, disheartened but determined. She realized that friendships, like life itself, undergo transitions. While Sarah had become a city girl, Emman had embraced her suburban roots. Instead of clinging to what they once had, they both needed to embrace their individual paths and accept the changes life had brought.

Over time, they learned to appreciate their differences. Sarah shared stories of her city adventures, and Emman spoke of the tranquil moments in the suburbs. They found common ground in their shared memories and their desire to support each other's unique journeys.

Their friendship transformed from what it once was into something new and different. It was no longer based on proximity or shared experiences but on a deep understanding and acceptance of each other's evolving lives.

In the end, Sarah and Emman discovered that even as life transitions change friendships, the truest bonds can adapt and thrive, evolving just as beautifully as the people who share them.

6. Jealousy or Competition: Negative feelings like jealousy or competition can damage a friendship.

Jealousy

Once upon a time in a quiet, picturesque village, there lived two inseparable friends, Lily and Sarah. They had been best friends since childhood, sharing every joy and sorrow. Their friendship was the envy of the entire village.

However, as they grew older, jealousy began to creep into Lily's heart. Sarah possessed a natural talent for painting, and her artwork was gaining recognition far and wide. Lily, on the other hand, struggled to find her passion and felt overshadowed by Sarah's success.

One fateful day, a renowned art critic visited their village and admired Sarah's paintings, praising her talent. Lily couldn't bear it any longer. Consumed by jealousy, she pretended to be happy for Sarah but secretly resented her success.

Lily's jealousy festered, and she started distancing herself from Sarah. They stopped spending as much time together, and the warmth in their friendship began to wane. Sarah noticed the change but couldn't understand why Lily was pulling away.

One evening, their strained relationship reached a breaking point. Sarah won a prestigious art competition, and the news spread like wildfire throughout the village. Lily's jealousy erupted into a bitter argument. Hurtful words were exchanged, and they parted ways, their beautiful friendship irreparably damaged.

Over time, both women regretted the way jealousy had poisoned their bond. They realized that their friendship had been more valuable than any success or recognition. Sadly, it was too late to mend the rift, and they went their separate ways, haunted by the memory of a once-beautiful friendship that had been spoiled by jealousy.

7. **Unresolved Issues:** Lingering unresolved issues can erode the foundation of a friendship.

Unresolved Issues

Once upon a time in a small, close-knit town, there lived two best friends, Dhristi and Mily. They had been inseparable since childhood, sharing secrets, dreams, and countless adventures. Their friendship was the envy of everyone around them, a shining example of what true companionship looked like.

However, as they grew older, life started to introduce new challenges. Dhristi was always punctual, organized, and preferred planning ahead. Mily, on the other hand, was more laid-back, spontaneous, and often late. Initially, these differences added a touch of excitement to their friendship. But over time, they became a source of frustration.

One sunny afternoon, Dhristi and Mily had plans to visit a nearby lake. Dhristi arrived on time, with a well-packed picnic basket and a detailed plan for the day. Mily, as usual, was running late. Dhristi, growing increasingly impatient, couldn't hide her irritation. When Mily finally arrived, she sensed Dhristi's anger but brushed it off with a careless laugh.

The day at the lake turned out to be less enjoyable than they had hoped. Dhristi's resentment simmered just below the surface, while Mily, oblivious to her friend's feelings, continued to act carefree. The unresolved tension hung over them like a storm cloud.

This incident was a turning point. Over the following weeks, Dhristi's frustration grew into resentment, while Mily couldn't understand what had changed. They started avoiding each other, canceling plans, and making excuses. The once-cherished bond between them began to wither.

Their mutual friends noticed the growing rift and tried to mediate, but neither Dhristi nor Mily was willing to confront the issues that were tearing them apart. They had invested so much in their friendship that admitting the problems felt like an admission of failure.

Months passed, and the silence between them became deafening. One day, Dhristi finally mustered the courage to send Mily a long, heartfelt message, pouring out her feelings and frustrations. Mily, surprised by the depth of Dhristi's emotions, responded with her own thoughts and concerns.

As they exchanged messages, it became clear that their friendship had been strained by a lack of communication and understanding. They both realized that they had been clinging to their past selves, failing to accept the changes that time had brought.

With tears and apologies, they decided to meet in person. They talked for hours, addressing their differences, apologizing for their mistakes, and vowing to communicate better in the future. Their friendship, once on the brink of collapse, slowly began to heal.

From that day forward, Dhristi and Mily made an effort to appreciate each other's strengths and accept their differences. They learned that unresolved issues, left to fester, could indeed kill even the strongest of friendships. But they also discovered that with open and honest communication, a damaged friendship could be revived and made even stronger.

It's important to remember that not all friendships will last forever, and that's okay. People change, circumstances change, and it's natural for friendships to evolve or end. What's crucial is to appreciate the friendships you have and work on maintaining them when possible.

New Beginning

Healing Hearts

Nisha had always been deeply in love with Anant. Their relationship had been a whirlwind of emotions, laughter, and shared dreams. They talked about a future together, but life had other plans. After several years, their relationship unraveled, leaving Nisha in emotional distress.

The breakup hit her hard. Nisha felt a profound sense of loss and loneliness. She found herself replaying memories of the good times they'd shared, unable to let go of the past. Her friends, especially her close friend Anurag, had been her pillars of support during these trying times.

Anurag had seen Nisha through the highs and lows of her relationship with Anant. He had always been the voice of reason, the one who encouraged her to pursue her dreams and maintain her independence. Seeing Nisha struggle with the breakup, Anurag knew she needed time to heal.

However, as Nisha grappled with the pain of her breakup, she unexpectedly crossed paths with someone new - a kind and understanding man named Anurag. He had known her for years, but in this moment of vulnerability, they grew closer.

Their friendship blossomed into something more. Anurag was patient and caring, helping Nisha navigate her emotional distress. He provided a shoulder to cry on and offered words of encouragement. Nisha found herself opening up to him in ways she hadn't with anyone else.

But as their relationship deepened, Nisha couldn't help but wonder if she was merely seeking solace in Anurag to escape the pain of her previous breakup. She felt conflicted about moving forward so soon, fearing that her emotions were still entangled with memories of Anant.

One evening, as they sat on Nisha's porch, Anurag gently took her hand and said, "Nisha, I care about you deeply, and I want to see you happy. But I also want you to heal fully from your past relationship before we take this any further. It's important that we both are emotionally ready for what lies ahead."

Nisha looked into Anurag's eyes, touched by his understanding and concern. She realized that he was right. She needed time to heal, to untangle her heart from the past. Anurag's patience and support had shown her that there could be a future, but rushing into it wasn't the answer.

Over time, Nisha and Anurag continued to grow closer as friends. Nisha took the necessary steps to mend her emotional wounds, and Anurag was there every step of the way. Their connection deepened, rooted in friendship and genuine care for each other.

Nisha eventually found herself in a place of emotional strength and clarity. She knew that her feelings for Anurag were genuine and not a mere escape from her past. Together, they embarked on a new chapter, one built on a foundation of trust, friendship, and the lessons learned from their past experiences.

Nisha's journey from emotional distress to a new relationship was a testament to the resilience of the human heart. She had learned that healing takes time and that true love can emerge when both partners are emotionally ready to embrace it.

A New Dawn

Once upon a time in a quiet suburban neighborhood, Arnav and Radhika were the talk of the town. Their love story was legendary, having met in college and grown inseparable over the years. For a decade, their love had remained unwavering, and they were the envy of their friends and family.

However, there was one aspect of their relationship that they had never quite managed to harmonize–physical intimacy. Despite their deep emotional connection, their physical compatibility had always been a challenge. This struggle led to frustration and moments of despair, both for Arnav and Radhika.

One fateful day, Arnav crossed paths with Nisha at a local coffee shop. Nisha was a kind and empathetic soul, who just happened to be a therapist specializing in couples counseling. She noticed Arnav's distant demeanor and struck up a conversation. Intrigued by her compassionate nature, Arnav found solace in confiding his marital issues to her.

As Arnav began attending counseling sessions with Nisha, their interactions grew more personal. Nisha's understanding and warmth created a unique bond between them. Arnav found himself drawn to her not just emotionally but also physically. He was torn between his enduring love for Radhika and his newfound connection with Nisha.

Arnav's dilemma raised questions about the nature of his relationship with Nisha. Was this emotional and physical connection with Nisha considered cheating on Radhika, despite his unresolved physical issues with his wife? It was a moral and emotional quandary that weighed heavily on his conscience.

Radhika, sensing a change in Arnav's behavior, confronted him one evening. Tearfully, he confessed to his deepening feelings for Nisha, not out of malice but as a result of seeking solace and understanding.

Radhika, hurt and confused, insisted they seek couples counseling together, determined to save their marriage. With the guidance of a skilled therapist, they embarked on a journey of self-discovery and healing, addressing both their physical and emotional challenges. It was a difficult process, filled with ups and downs, but their love for each other remained the driving force.

As for Nisha, she recognized the importance of professional boundaries and the ethical dilemma she had inadvertently become a part of. She decided to distance herself from Arnav and focus solely on her role as a therapist, helping other couples navigate their own challenges.

In the end, Arnav and Radhika's marriage faced the ultimate test, and they emerged stronger and more united than ever. Their story served as a reminder that love, even when faced with challenges, can overcome obstacles when both partners are committed to open communication, understanding, and, above all, honesty.

Beyond Boundaries

Nishant and Tanya had built a life together that was filled with love, trust, and understanding. Their 20-year marriage had seen its fair share of ups and downs, but their commitment to each other had always prevailed. They had raised three wonderful children, who were now grown up and forging their paths in the world.

Nishant had always known about his sexual preferences, and he had been honest with Tanya about it from the beginning.

She, in turn, had shown incredible compassion and support for him. They had discussed the challenges that Nishant's sexual orientation might pose to their marriage, and together, they had decided to navigate it with open hearts and minds.

Over the years, Nishant and Tanya had continued to grow closer, not just as partners but as best friends. They had explored ways to maintain their emotional and physical connection, finding new dimensions of intimacy that went beyond traditional boundaries.

Nishant had occasionally met other men, but he had always been transparent with Tanya about these encounters. They had established clear boundaries and communicated openly about their feelings, ensuring that trust remained the cornerstone of their relationship.

For Nishant, the question of whether sleeping with other men was considered cheating had always been about context and communication. Tanya, with her fair understanding of the situation, had never viewed it as betrayal because they had defined their rules within the confines of their marriage.

As time went on, Nishant and Tanya continued to cherish their unique bond, proving that love could indeed conquer the most challenging circumstances. They were a testament to the power of open communication, trust, and unconditional acceptance, showing the world that love could thrive in the face of adversity and societal norms.

Love Beyond Secrets

Nishi had always lived a double life. By day, she was a charming and talented artist, admired by many in her community for her creativity and talent. By night, she had another identity - a call girl. It was a secret she had kept hidden from everyone, a way to make ends meet while pursuing her true passion.

One fateful evening, Nishi was introduced to a new client, Raj, a successful businessman. Little did she know that this encounter would change her life forever. Raj's warmth and kindness struck a chord with Nishi, and over the course of their meetings, they began to form a deep connection that went beyond their initial arrangement.

As their relationship deepened, Nishi found herself falling in love with Raj. To her surprise, she discovered that he felt the same way about her. Their love was undeniable, but Nishi couldn't shake the guilt of her secret life. She knew that honesty was the foundation of any lasting relationship, but revealing the truth about her profession was a daunting prospect.

One evening, as they sat together on the rooftop of Nishi's apartment, the city lights twinkling below, Nishi mustered the courage to speak. "Raj," she began, her voice trembling slightly, "there's something I need to tell you."

Raj looked at her, his eyes filled with concern. "What is it, Nishi? You can tell me anything."

With a deep breath, Nishi confessed her secret, her voice quivering as she laid bare the truth about her night-time occupation. She expected shock, judgment, or even rejection, but Raj surprised her with his response. He listened attentively, his expression a mix of emotions.

When she finished, Raj took her hands in his and said, "Nishi, thank you for trusting me with this. I won't pretend it's easy to hear, but I love you for your honesty. What you do to make a living doesn't define who you are."

Tears welled up in Nishi's eyes as she realized the depth of Raj's love and acceptance. It was a pivotal moment in their relationship, one that strengthened the bond between them.

Over time, Raj and Nishi faced challenges together, supporting each other through the ups and downs of life. Nishi eventually found the courage to leave her double life behind, pursuing her art and other fulfilling opportunities.

Their love story became a testament to the power of honesty, acceptance, and the capacity of two people to love each other despite their differences. Nishi and Raj's relationship thrived, proving that true love could conquer even the most unexpected obstacles life threw their way.

Unbreakable Bonds

Raj sat in his study, his world shattered by Priti's revelation. His mind raced as he grappled with the truth that their only son was not biologically his. The weight of the moment pressed upon him, but his love for his family remained steadfast.

He decided to have an honest conversation with Priti. They needed to understand why she had kept this secret for so long. The truth, he knew, had the power to heal or harm. They sat down together, their hearts heavy with the weight of their shared history.

Priti, her eyes filled with regret, explained how, years ago, she had been in a difficult situation. She had faced the unimaginable choice of revealing the truth and potentially breaking their family apart or keeping the secret to protect their son from a complicated truth.

Raj, though hurt and confused, recognized the love and sacrifice in Priti's actions. He understood the depths of her love for both him and their son. After hours of conversation, tears, and reflection, they decided that love would guide their next steps.

Raj embraced his son and assured him that being a father wasn't about biology but about love and commitment. He knew that biology didn't define a family; love, trust, and understanding did.

As they navigated the challenges of this newfound truth, Raj and Priti's love grew stronger. They decided to amend their will together, leaving their son an equal share of their love and support. Raj learned that family was more than blood, and that the bonds they shared were unbreakable.

Their story became a testament to the enduring power of love and the resilience of a family forged through both truth and forgiveness.

Infidelity in Relationships

Raj and Maya had been together for what felt like a lifetime. Their love story had started in college, blossoming into a deep and enduring connection. They were the kind of couple that everyone admired - the couple that seemed inseparable. However, like any relationship, theirs had its challenges.

As the years passed, life's demands began to pull them in different directions. Raj was climbing the corporate ladder, working late into the night to secure their financial future. Maya, on the other hand, was pursuing her passion for art, often traveling to workshops and exhibitions. The space between them grew, and they drifted apart emotionally.

One fateful evening, Raj found himself working late again. Feeling lonely and neglected, he sought solace in the company of a coworker, Sarah. They began spending more time together, sharing their frustrations about their respective relationships. One thing led to another, and Raj and Sarah found themselves entangled in an affair.

Meanwhile, Maya sensed the growing distance between her and Raj. She tried to rekindle their connection, suggesting weekend getaways and date nights, but Raj always had an excuse. Frustration and suspicion gnawed at her, leading her to confide in her best friend, Lisa.

Lisa, who had experienced infidelity in her own past, advised Maya to trust her instincts and dig deeper. Maya reluctantly started looking for clues and soon discovered text messages and emails between Raj and Sarah that left no room for doubt. Heartbroken, she confronted Raj, who confessed to his affair.

The revelation shattered Maya. She couldn't believe that the man she had loved and trusted for so long had betrayed her. Raj was remorseful and begged for forgiveness, promising to end the affair and work on their relationship. But the damage was done, and Maya couldn't easily forget or forgive.

Their relationship entered a tumultuous phase of anger, hurt, and therapy sessions. Maya faced a difficult decision - whether to try to rebuild the shattered trust or to end the relationship that had defined her adult life. It was a painful journey of introspection and healing for both Raj and Maya, with no easy answers.

In the end, Raj's infidelity became a turning point in their lives. Whether they chose to salvage their relationship or part ways, they knew that they had to confront their own shortcomings and desires, ultimately rediscovering what love and commitment meant to each of them.

Right or Wrong

Once upon a time in a bustling city, there lived a woman named Manju. She had a loving husband named Ashok, and together they had built a beautiful life with two grown-up children. Their family seemed picture-perfect to those who knew them.

Manju was a dedicated employee at a thriving company, where she worked alongside a young and charismatic coworker named Vicky. Vicky, ten years her junior, was not only charming but also incredibly talented. His youthful exuberance and zest for life drew Manju towards him.

As days turned into weeks and weeks into months, Manju and Vicky found themselves spending more and more time together. What started as innocent conversations at the office soon blossomed into a deep connection neither of them had anticipated. Manju couldn't help but be drawn to Vicky's vitality, and Vicky was captivated by Manju's wisdom and grace.

Manju's heart became divided between two worlds. She loved Ashok deeply, appreciating the years they had spent together, the memories they had created, and the family they had built. Yet, she couldn't deny the intense affection she felt for Vicky. It was a love that seemed to transcend age and logic.

Caught in the midst of this emotional turmoil, Manju found herself torn between her loyalty to her husband and her passionate feelings for Vicky. She knew that her actions had the potential to shatter the life she had built with Ashok and their children, but she couldn't simply ignore the emotions that had taken hold of her.

As the story unfolds, Manju faces a difficult decision. Should she follow her heart and risk everything for a new, passionate love with Vicky, or should she choose to honor her commitment to Ashok and the family they had built together? In this complex web of emotions, the choices she makes will shape the lives of those around her and ultimately reveal the true depths of her character.

Manju reached a crossroads in her life, torn between her love for Ashok and Vicky. However, she couldn't bear to choose one over the other, believing that love couldn't be measured or confined to simple choices. She made a difficult decision to leave both Ashok and Vicky, hoping to find her own path and rediscover herself.

With a heavy heart, she sat down with Ashok, her husband of many years, and Vicky, her passionate affair, and explained her decision. Tears were shed, emotions ran high, but Manju knew it was the only way she could stay true to her beliefs about love.

Walking away from both relationships was a painful journey for Manju. She embarked on a path of self-discovery, seeking to understand the complexities of love and the choices she had made. It was a challenging road, but she hoped that in time, she would find a deeper understanding of what love truly meant to her.

As Manju ventured into the unknown, she carried the lessons learned from her past loves, cherishing the memories she had shared with Ashok and Vicky. While her story took an unconventional turn, it was a testament to her belief that love was boundless and couldn't always fit within the confines of societal norms. Manju's journey became a reminder that love, in all its forms, could be a force that reshaped lives and pushed people to explore the boundaries of their own hearts.

Love Beyond Boundaries

Once upon a time in a quaint town, there lived Nilay and Nimish, two souls deeply in love. They had known each other since childhood, and their bond had blossomed into a profound love that knew no bounds. However, they were well aware of the cultural and societal barriers that stood in the way of their love.

Solution 1: The Secret Love

Nilay and Nimish decided to keep their love a secret from their families. They met in hidden places, wrote secret love letters, and cherished stolen moments. This clandestine love continued for years, providing them with happiness but also a sense of longing for acceptance.

Solution 2: The Persuasive Approach

Nilay and Nimish decided to confront their families with their love. They believed that if they could eloquently express their feelings and the strength of their relationship, their families might come around. They embarked on a journey to gather support from friends and mentors who could help mediate the conversation with their families.

Solution 3: The Relocation

Realizing the challenges of societal expectations, Nilay and Nimish contemplated moving to a more accepting place where they could live openly as a couple without fear of judgment. They began researching cities and countries that were known for their diverse and inclusive communities.

Solution 4: The Slow Change

Nilay and Nimish decided to focus on changing their families' perceptions over time. They continued their relationship while also working on projects and activities that demonstrated their commitment and love. They hoped that by showcasing their love through their actions, their families would eventually come to accept them.

Solution 5: The Compromise

In a last-ditch effort to gain acceptance from their families, Nilay and Nimish considered compromising on some aspects of their relationship. They knew it wouldn't be easy, but they were willing to make adjustments to honor their families' values while also preserving their love.

As the story unfolds, the paths Nilay and Nimish choose will lead them on different journeys, each filled with its own challenges and triumphs. The ultimate question for them remains: Can love truly conquer all, or will they be forced to make sacrifices for the sake of societal norms and family expectations?

Should they get married as per family wishes and continue their hidden relationship

The decision of whether Nilay and Nimish should get married as per their family's wishes while continuing their hidden relationship is a complex one, and it ultimately depends on their personal values, priorities, and the specific circumstances of their situation. Here are some considerations:

Family Expectations: If both Nilay and Nimish highly value family harmony and are willing to make sacrifices for the sake of their families' happiness, getting married as per their families' wishes might seem like a viable option.

Long-Term Consequences: They should carefully consider the potential long-term consequences of this decision. Will they be content with a loveless or hidden marriage? Can they sustain this arrangement without causing harm to themselves or their families emotionally?

Authenticity: On the other hand, they may feel that living a life that is not true to their authentic selves is emotionally damaging. Continuing a hidden relationship after marriage might lead to feelings of guilt and deceit.

Communication: Open and honest communication between Nilay and Nimish is crucial. They need to discuss their feelings, fears, and the impact of such a decision on their mental and emotional well-being.

Alternative Solutions: Before making such a significant decision, they could explore alternative solutions, such as seeking support from friends, family, or counselors who may help bridge the gap between their love and their families' expectations.

Ultimately, Nilay and Nimish should carefully weigh the pros and cons of getting married as per their family's wishes while continuing their hidden relationship. They should also consider the impact on their own happiness and well-being. Love is a powerful force, but it must be balanced with practical considerations and individual values.

Naman and Maya's Perspective:

Naman:

At 65, I never expected to feel the warmth of love again. Life had dealt me its share of joys and sorrows, and I had resigned myself to solitude after losing my beloved wife. But fate had different plans. One fateful day, I met Maya, a vibrant 60-year-old woman with a heart full of kindness. Her laughter was like music, and her smile could brighten even the darkest of days. Without realizing that our children were dating, I fell head over heels for her.

Maya:

Meeting Naman was like discovering a long-lost treasure. His wisdom and gentleness drew me in like a moth to a flame. We shared stories of our past, our dreams, and found solace in each other's company. Little did we know that our children, who had met through a chance encounter, were growing closer every day. Naman and I decided to take the plunge, believing that love had found us again, never suspecting the intricate web of connections that fate had woven.

Their Kids' Perspective:

Sara (Naman's Daughter):

When I introduced my boyfriend, Raj, to my dad, Naman, I never expected to see that look of shock and disbelief on his face. It turns out Raj's mom, Maya, was the woman Dad had been seeing. Our secret relationship was exposed, and we faced a dilemma: How do we tell our parents about us without hurting them?

Raj (Maya's Son):

Meeting Sara felt like destiny. We fell in love, unaware that our parents were also falling for each other. The guilt of hiding our relationship weighed on us. We had to come clean to our parents and face the consequences. It was a tough conversation, but we knew our love was worth it.

Society's Perspective:

Society:

Whispers began to circulate in our close-knit community as news of Naman and Maya's relationship spread. Some raised their eyebrows, skeptical of love blossoming in the twilight years. Others embraced the idea, celebrating the second chances life had to offer. The real shock came when Sara and

Raj revealed their relationship, causing a wave of mixed reactions. Some saw it as a peculiar twist of fate, while others criticized the secrecy.

As the two couples navigated their intertwined destinies, society learned valuable lessons about love, acceptance, and the unpredictable nature of life. In the end, love conquered all, proving that age and unexpected connections couldn't stand in the way of genuine feelings.

Complex Love

Siddharth: (Nervously) Mitali, there's something important I need to talk to you about.

Mitali: (Curious but concerned) What is it, Siddharth? You seem really serious.

Siddharth: (Pauses) Mitali, I've been struggling with something for a long time, and I don't know how to say this, but... I'm gay.

Mitali: (Surprised and emotional) Oh, Siddharth, thank you for trusting me with this. It must have been really hard for you to tell me.

Siddharth: (Tearfully) It was, Mitali. I didn't want to hurt you, but I couldn't keep this from you any longer.

Mitali: (Taking a deep breath) Siddharth, I appreciate your honesty, but I also have to be honest with you. I don't think it's fair to either of us if we continue a romantic relationship when you have this realization about your sexual orientation.

Siddharth: (Looking sad) I understand what you're saying, Mitali. But I want to try to make this work, to see if we can still have a meaningful relationship.

Mitali: (Touched but firm) Siddharth, I care about you deeply, and I want you to be happy. But I also don't want either of us to be trapped in a relationship that might not fulfill our needs. It's important for both of us to find the love and happiness we deserve.

Siddharth: (Resigned) I know you're right, Mitali. I just hoped that we could make it work somehow.

Mitali: (Gently) Siddharth, our friendship and connection will always be there. But sometimes, we have to let go of one path to find another that leads to our true happiness.

Siddharth: (Tearfully) Thank you for understanding, Mitali. I'll always cherish what we had.

Mitali: (Holding back tears) And I'll always be here for you, Siddharth, as a friend who cares deeply about your happiness.

(They share a heartfelt, bittersweet moment, knowing that this difficult conversation is a step toward a more authentic future for both of them.)

Several years later:

Mitali: (Feeling uneasy) Siddharth, we've been through so much together, and I thought we had an understanding about your sexual orientation. But recently, I've been hearing rumors and feeling like something's not right. Are you having an affair with another man?

Siddharth: (Avoiding eye contact, hesitant) Mitali, I'm so sorry. Yes, I am. I've been seeing someone, and it's a man. I didn't know how to tell you, and I didn't want to hurt you again.

Mitali: (Feeling hurt and betrayed) Siddharth, I appreciate your honesty, but this hurts so much. We agreed to try and make our relationship work, and now you're seeing someone else behind my back.

Siddharth: (Regretful) I know, Mitali, and I'm truly sorry. I thought I could suppress my feelings and make it work, but it became too difficult for me.

Mitali: (Tears welling up) Siddharth, it's not just about you. It's about the trust we had and the commitment we made to each other. This hurts deeply, and it's hard to see a future together when you've broken that trust.

Siddharth: (Sincere) I understand if you can't forgive me, Mitali. I never wanted to hurt you like this.

Mitali: (Taking a deep breath) Siddharth, I need time to think about what I want and what's best for both of us. This is a lot to process, and I don't want to make any hasty decisions.

(They part ways, both with heavy hearts, uncertain about the future of their relationship.)

What if Siddharth and Mitali agree to continue with their relationship like this only cause they love each other

Mitali: Siddharth, I know it's complicated, but I love you, and I don't want to lose you.

Siddharth: Mitali, I love you too, and I don't want to lose you either. We've been through so much together, and I don't want to give up on us.

Siddharth: (Holding Mitali's hand) Maybe we can find a way to make this work. We can be open about my feelings and your concerns, and we'll support each other.

Mitali: (Smiling through tears) Yes, let's be honest with each other and communicate better. Love can conquer many challenges, Siddharth, and I believe in us.

(They decide to continue their relationship, knowing it won't be easy, but their love and commitment to each other give them hope for a future together.)

Bittersweet Choices

In a bustling city where dreams converged and relationships were as complex as the streets themselves, there lived Shrang and Abhay. They were in a relationship that seemed perfect on the surface, but beneath the façade, cracks ran deep.

Shrang was charismatic, the center of attention in his circle of friends. He was known as the ultimate women charmer, and his reputation meant the world to him. However, behind closed doors, he was controlling and often stifled Abhay's voice, especially in front of his friends. Abhay, on the other hand, was gentle and kind-hearted, deeply in love with Shrang, but the weight of silence was becoming unbearable.

One summer evening, Shrang invited his friends over for a rooftop party. Abhay watched as Shrang effortlessly charmed the group with his witty banter and charismatic smile. When Abhay attempted to join the conversation, Shrang's stern look silenced him. Abhay's eyes filled with pain, but he dared not express his feelings in front of Shrang's friends.

As the weeks passed, Abhay felt increasingly isolated. Shrang was never available when Abhay needed him, often citing work or other commitments. Yet, when Abhay tried to talk about his loneliness and emotional turmoil, Shrang emotionally blackmailed him, reminding him of all the good times they had shared.

One fateful day, Abhay's world was shrouded in despair. He stood on the edge of a bridge, contemplating suicide, unable to bear the emotional turmoil any longer. Just as he was about to take a step forward, a stranger named Nishant intervened.

Their eyes met, and in that moment, something profound happened.

Nishant, with his warm smile and empathetic soul, showed Abhay kindness and understanding that he had never experienced before. They began to spend time together, sharing their hopes, dreams, and fears. Abhay found solace in Nishant's presence, and gradually, their friendship blossomed into love.

However, Abhay was torn. He still loved Shrang, despite the pain and control he had endured. He didn't want to hurt Shrang, and the emotional entanglement left him in a state of constant conflict.

One evening, Abhay mustered the courage to confront Shrang about his feelings for Nishant. Shrang, taken aback, finally realized the depth of Abhay's pain. He promised to change, to be more supportive and loving. But Abhay had tasted the sweetness of freedom with Nishant, and he couldn't ignore his newfound love.

In the end, Abhay chose to be true to himself and pursue a future with Nishant, despite the heartache it would bring to both him and Shrang. Love, he learned, should be liberating and not a chain that suffocates. As Abhay walked away, he carried the bittersweet memories of his past love with Shrang, knowing that his heart would forever be divided between two chapters of his life.

Can a person like Shrang change?

Yes, it is possible for a person like Shrang to change, but it depends on various factors, including their willingness to change, self-awareness, and the support they receive. People can change their behavior and attitudes if they recognize the need for change and are motivated to do so.

In Shrang's case, if he realizes the harm his controlling and manipulative behaviour has caused in his relationship with Abhay and genuinely desires to improve, he can seek therapy or counselling to work on his issues. Self-reflection and a commitment to personal growth can lead to positive changes in a person's behaviour and outlook.

However, it's important to note that change can be challenging and may take time. It also requires consistent effort and a sincere desire to become a better person. The extent to which Shrang can change depends on his own determination and the support he receives from those around him.

Is it worth for Abhay waiting for Shrang to change which is a big question mark cause Shrang feels he can't be wrong?

Deciding whether it's worth waiting for someone to change, especially when they are unwilling to acknowledge their faults, can be a difficult and deeply personal decision. Here are some considerations for Abhay:

1. Self-Respect: Abhay should prioritize his own well-being and self-respect. If waiting for Shrang to change means enduring ongoing emotional pain, control, and manipulation, it may not be healthy for Abhay.

2. Communication: Abhay should have an open and honest conversation with Shrang about his feelings and concerns. It's essential for Shrang to understand the impact of his behaviour on Abhay.

3. Realistic Expectations: Abhay should assess whether Shrang is genuinely committed to changing and improving the relationship. If Shrang is unwilling to acknowledge his faults or shows no genuine effort to change, waiting for change might be futile.

4. Personal Growth: Abhay should focus on his own personal growth and happiness. It may involve seeking support from friends, family, or professionals to navigate the challenges of the relationship.

5. Time Frame: If Abhay decides to give Shrang a chance to change, he should set realistic time frames and boundaries. It's important not to allow the waiting period to become indefinite.

Ultimately, Abhay should prioritize his own well-being and happiness. If he feels that waiting for Shrang to change is causing more harm than good, it might be necessary to consider moving on and seeking a healthier and more fulfilling relationship elsewhere. Every situation is unique, and Abhay's decision should be based on what he believes is in his best interest.

Journey of Karmic Connections

Few relations come in one's life with a time limit because they are your karmic connections – few things which you are supposed to finish in this journey of life.

Karmic connections are a concept rooted in various spiritual and philosophical traditions, suggesting that our relationships and experiences in life are shaped by past actions or karma.

1. Karma and Connections: Karmic connections imply that people come into our lives for a reason, often related to unfinished business or lessons from past lives. These connections can be intense and meaningful, but they might not last a lifetime.

2. Lessons and Growth: Karmic connections often serve as a means for personal growth and spiritual development. These

relationships can challenge us, helping us learn important life lessons or resolve past conflicts.

3. Temporary Nature: Karmic connections may indeed have a time limit. Once the intended lesson or purpose has been fulfilled, these relationships may naturally drift apart or end, and this can be a source of emotional pain and confusion.

4. Acceptance and Closure: Accepting the temporary nature of these connections can lead to closure and a deeper understanding of life's intricate web. It's important to acknowledge that not all relationships are meant to last forever.

5. Free Will and Choice: While karmic connections may bring people into our lives, our free will and choices also play a significant role in how these relationships unfold. We can choose to learn from them, resolve issues, or move on.

6. Healing and Forgiveness: Sometimes, karmic connections involve healing old wounds or forgiving past actions. By doing so, we can break free from cycles of karma and create more positive energy in our lives.

7. Continuing the Journey: After a karmic connection ends, it's essential to continue our life's journey with an open heart and mind. New relationships and experiences await, each with its unique purpose.

Karmic connections are those relationships that come into our lives with a specific purpose, often related to past actions or karma. Recognizing and understanding the temporary nature of these connections can help us navigate them with greater awareness and acceptance, ultimately contributing to our personal growth and spiritual evolution.

Healing from Karmic Connections and Forgiving Them

Let's explore the concept of healing and forgiveness in karmic relationships through the story of two friends, Anand and Nikunj:

Anand and Nikunj had been best friends since childhood. They shared countless memories and experiences, and their bond was unbreakable. However, as they grew older, conflicts began to arise between them. Small misunderstandings turned into bigger arguments, and their friendship started to deteriorate.

Unbeknownst to them, their relationship was a karmic connection. In past lives, they had been close friends who had experienced a painful betrayal. The unresolved karma from that past life was affecting their current relationship, causing tension and conflict.

As their friendship reached a breaking point, Anand and Nikunj decided to seek guidance from a spiritual mentor who explained the concept of karmic relationships to them. They learned that their clashes reflected the past karma they needed to resolve. This realization was a turning point in their journey.

Anand and Nikunj decided to embark on a journey of healing and forgiveness. They acknowledged the pain they had caused each other and the wounds they carried from their past life. Through open and honest communication, they shared their feelings and fears, allowing deep emotions to surface.

Forgiveness played a crucial role in their healing process. They forgave each other for the hurt they had inflicted and themselves for holding onto grudges for so long. This act of forgiveness was liberating, releasing the negative energy that had bound them in a cycle of conflict.

Slowly but steadily, Anand and Nikunj's friendship began to transform. As they let go of their past grievances and actively worked on healing their relationship, a sense of peace and understanding enveloped them. Their bond grew stronger than ever before.

Through their journey of healing and forgiveness, Anand and Nikunj not only repaired their friendship but also resolved the karmic connection that had plagued them for lifetimes. They learned that karmic relationships could provide opportunities for growth, but it's up to individuals to choose healing and forgiveness to break free from past patterns.

Their story serves as a beautiful example of how confronting past karma with understanding, forgiveness, and love can lead to profound healing and transformation in karmic relationships.

What if Anand doesn't believe in past life and karmic connections, can Nikunj do it on his own?

If Anand doesn't believe in past lives and karmic connections, it may complicate the process of resolving their karmic relationship solely through that framework. However, Nikunj can still work on improving the relationship and seeking resolution to past conflicts to some extent, even if Anand doesn't share the same belief. Here's how:

1. Open Communication: Nikunj can have an open and honest conversation with Anand about their friendship's challenges and the desire to mend their relationship. Even if Anand doesn't believe in past lives or karma, he may still be willing to discuss and address their current issues.

2. Focus on the Present: Instead of discussing past lives or karmic connections, Nikunj can emphasize the importance of the present moment and their current feelings. He can express

his desire to make their friendship better moving forward, regardless of past beliefs.

3. Apologize and Forgive: Nikunj can take the initiative to apologize for any actions or words that have hurt Anand and express his willingness to forgive Anand for any past grievances. This can be done without invoking the concept of karma.

4. Seek Professional Help: If the conflicts between Anand and Nikunj are deep-seated and challenging to resolve on their own, they may consider seeking the guidance of a therapist or counsellor who can help them navigate their relationship issues without necessarily involving spiritual beliefs.

5. Lead by Example: Nikunj can lead by example by demonstrating positive changes in the way he interacts with Anand. By showing kindness, empathy, and a commitment to improving their friendship, he may inspire Anand to do the same.

While Anand's disbelief in past lives and karmic connections may limit the scope of using that framework for resolving their relationship issues, Nikunj can still take steps to work on their friendship and seek resolution through open communication, forgiveness, and a focus on the present. Ultimately, the success of improving their relationship will depend on both individuals' willingness to engage in the process, regardless of their spiritual beliefs.

Tale of Communication and Understanding

Once upon a time in a bustling city, Sara and James were deeply in love. They had been together for a few years and shared countless memories. However, as time passed, a subtle imbalance started to creep into their relationship.

Sara noticed that when she needed emotional support or just someone to talk to during her tough times, James was often unavailable. He was always preoccupied with work commitments, which he took very seriously. On the other hand, when James needed her to be there for him, he expected her undivided attention, and it left Sara feeling like a parasite, as though she only existed to meet his needs.

One evening, after a particularly frustrating day for Sara, she decided it was time to address the issue. She invited James to a quiet cafe, a place they had visited on their first date, where they had shared their dreams and fears.

With a steaming cup of coffee in hand, Sara looked into James's eyes and said, "James, I love you, and I want us to be there for each other, like we used to be. But lately, it feels like you're distant when I need you, and I feel overwhelmed. Yet, you expect my full attention when you're going through something. I don't want our relationship to become one sided."

James paused for a moment, taking in Sara's words. He realized he had been so caught up in his work that he hadn't been attentive to Sara's needs. He replied, "Sara, I'm sorry. I didn't realize I was neglecting you. I've been so focused on my job that I lost sight of what's important. You mean the world to me, and I want to make this right."

Together, they came up with a solution. They decided to set aside dedicated time for each other, to listen and support one another's dreams and challenges. They also agreed to communicate their needs and expectations more clearly.

As the months passed, Sara and James worked on their relationship diligently. They found a healthy balance between their personal and professional lives, ensuring that they were there for each other when it mattered most. Their love grew stronger, and they learned that true love isn't about being a parasite or being unavailable but about being partners who support and cherish each other through all of life's ups and downs.

In the end, Sara and James's love story became a testament to the power of communication and understanding in building a lasting and fulfilling relationship.

Journey to Fulfilment

In a cozy suburban neighborhood, Seema and Jatin had been married for two decades. Their love story was one of resilience and companionship, surviving the tests of time. They had a vibrant 10-year-old daughter named Mily, who brought endless joy to their lives.

As their anniversary approached, Seema couldn't shake the nagging feeling that something was amiss in their marriage. She found herself pondering this on the nights when Jatin was away on business trips or when she attended out-of-town meetings. Seema was grateful for Jatin's unwavering support in her career, for he always took charge of parenting duties and managed the household without a hint of complaint. His devotion to their family was unquestionable.

Yet, Seema's restlessness persisted. She confided in her closest friends, who suggested counselling and self-reflection. Seema, however, couldn't pinpoint the source of her discontent. She often gazed at Jatin, who remained the best husband and father she could ever wish for. He had given her the space to grow independently and had provided financial stability that allowed her to pursue her dreams.

One evening, as Seema returned from yet another business trip, she found Jatin and Mily engrossed in a board game.

Their laughter filled the house, and it warmed her heart. But there it was again – that persistent feeling that something was missing, that a piece of their puzzle was lost.

Over time, Seema realized that her dissatisfaction wasn't about what Jatin lacked as a husband and father; it was an internal struggle, a quest for something she couldn't quite define. She decided to embark on a journey of self-discovery, hoping to understand herself better.

Jatin, sensing his wife's restlessness, offered his unwavering support, just as he always had. He encouraged Sarah to take the time she needed to find herself, even if it meant being apart for a while. In this act of understanding and love, Seema discovered that the missing piece was her own sense of fulfilment, a passion that was uniquely hers.

As she pursued her dreams and passions, she realized that her marriage with Jatin was indeed perfect, not because it lacked flaws, but because it had weathered every storm together. Seema had grown independently, yet she had a partner who was always there for her and their family.

In the end, Seema's journey of self-discovery not only deepened her appreciation for Jatin but also rekindled the spark in their marriage. She understood that the missing piece was within her all along, and it was her responsibility to fill it with her own aspirations and passions. Together, they continued their journey as a loving couple, cherishing the imperfectly perfect life they had built together.

As a friend, how will you advise Seema when she comes to you saying that she feel something is missing in the relationship and she wants to end of this relationship with her husband Jatin

If Seema came to me as a friend expressing her feelings that something is missing in her relationship with her husband Jatin and that she's contemplating ending the relationship, I would approach the conversation with empathy and care. Here's how I might advise her:

1. **Listen Actively:** I would start by listening attentively to Seema's concerns without judgment. I'd encourage her to open up about her feelings and what specifically she thinks is missing in the relationship.

2. **Encourage Self-Reflection:** I'd suggest that Seema take some time for self-reflection. Often, it's important to understand whether the issue lies within oneself or within the relationship. Is there something specific she needs or wants that isn't being fulfilled, or is it a more generalized feeling of discontent?

3. **Seek Professional Help:** If Seema is unsure about her feelings or if the relationship issues seem complex, I'd recommend that she consider couples therapy or counselling. A trained therapist can provide valuable insights and help both partners communicate better.

4. **Consider the Long Term: ** I would advise Seema to think about the long-term implications of her decision. What are the consequences for her, Jatin, and their daughter? Sometimes, taking a step back and evaluating the bigger picture can provide clarity.

5. **Communication is Key:** Suggest that Seema openly communicates her feelings and concerns with Jatin. Honest and respectful communication can often lead to solutions or compromises that can improve the relationship.

6. **Prioritize Personal Growth: ** Encourage Sarah to focus on her personal growth and happiness, regardless of the

relationship's outcome. It's essential for her to be fulfilled as an individual.

7. **Be Patient: ** Decisions about ending a long-term relationship shouldn't be rushed. I'd remind her that it's okay to take time to make such a significant choice.

8. **Consider the Impact on Their Child: ** If Seema has concerns about their child, I'd emphasize the importance of ensuring a stable and supportive environment for her daughter, whether within the marriage or as co-parents if they decide to separate.

Ultimately, the decision to end or continue a marriage is deeply personal and should be made after careful consideration. My role as a friend would be to support Seema throughout this process, providing her with guidance and a listening ear, while respecting her autonomy in making choices about her own life and happiness.

Points

1. Seema and Jatin's enduring marriage faced a subtle imbalance as Seema felt something was missing despite Jatin's unwavering support.

2. Despite being an ideal husband and father, Jatin couldn't alleviate Seema's persistent restlessness.

3. Seema embarked on a journey of self-discovery to understand the source of her discontent.

4. Jatin, sensing Seema's restlessness, supported her decision to take time for self-discovery, highlighting his understanding and love.

5. Seema realized her dissatisfaction wasn't about Jatin's shortcomings but her internal struggle and quest for personal fulfilment.

6. Pursuing her dreams, Seema discovered the missing piece within herself and rekindled the spark in their marriage.

7. Their imperfectly perfect life became a testament to the power of understanding, support, and personal growth in a long-lasting relationship.

Journey to Self-Discovery

Vasundhara and Jai had been in a seemingly perfect relationship for five years. They shared laughter, dreams, and what Vasundhara thought was love. However, as time went on, Vasundhara began to notice subtle signs that something was amiss.

It started with little things - Jai becoming distant, canceling plans at the last minute, and always being elusive about his feelings. Vasundhara couldn't help but feel that Jai was emotionally distant, yet she hoped that things would get better with time.

Despite her concerns, Vasundhara loved Jai deeply and was emotionally invested in their relationship. She didn't want to admit that her five-year commitment might have been based on a lie. But the evidence was becoming increasingly difficult to ignore.

One day, Vasundhara decided it was time to confront Jai about her feelings. She gathered her courage and initiated a heartfelt conversation. Tears welled up in her eyes as she admitted her fear that Jai's love might not be genuine.

Jai hesitated for a moment, then finally confessed. He admitted that he had never truly loved Vasundhara, and their relationship had been convenient for him. He confessed that he had an emotional hold on her because he knew she was deeply in love with him.

Vasundhara was shattered. Her heart ached with the realization that she had wasted five years of her life on a relationship built on deceit. But she knew she had to regain control of her life and emotions.

First, Vasundhara decided to distance herself from Jai. She needed time to heal and rediscover her self-worth. She leaned on her friends and family for support, seeking their advice and love during this difficult time.

As time passed, Vasundhara began to rebuild her life. She focused on her own happiness, pursued her interests, and nurtured her self-esteem. She realized that her worth wasn't tied to Jai's approval or love.

Gradually, Vasundhara found the strength to let go of Jai completely. She knew that staying in a fake relationship was only holding her back from true happiness. With newfound clarity, she severed all ties with Jai and started on a journey of self-discovery.

It wasn't easy, but Vasundhara learned that her emotional well-being was more important than any relationship. She vowed never to allow someone to have that kind of emotional control over her again. Over time, she found genuine love and happiness, not just with someone new but within herself.

Vasundhara's story serves as a reminder that even in the darkest moments of heartbreak, one can find the strength to rebuild their life and find genuine love and happiness.

Unravelling Dreams

Once upon a time in a quiet suburban neighborhood, Nivedita and Anuj had invested their hard-earned money in buying their dream house. It was a charming, cozy place with a white picket fence and a garden filled with blooming roses. For years, it was the symbol of their love and shared dreams.

However, as time passed, their marriage started to crumble. They found themselves at odds with each other, unable to communicate or compromise. Amidst the chaos of their failing relationship, the issue of house possession became a major point of contention.

One evening, while sitting in the living room they had once lovingly decorated together, Nivedita spoke up. "Anuj, I think we need to figure out what to do with the house. It's causing us more stress than anything else."

Anuj nodded, realizing that holding onto the house was a source of emotional pain for both. They decided to seek professional advice to navigate this difficult situation.

They met with a financial counselor who provided valuable insights. The counselor suggested that they consider selling the house and dividing the proceeds equally. This way, they could each move forward with their lives independently, free from the emotional baggage associated with the house.

While making this decision, they also reflected on their finances and whether it was okay for couples to handle their finances independently. They came to the realization that, while it's important to share financial goals and have open discussions about money, it's also crucial to maintain some financial independence. This way, each person can have a sense of autonomy and security.

In the end, Nivedita and Anuj sold their dream house. They divided the proceeds fairly and started new chapters in their lives. They learned that handling finances independently, to some extent, can be a healthy way to ensure individual financial well-being and reduce potential conflicts in a relationship.

Their story serves as a reminder that sometimes letting go of material possessions can lead to greater emotional and financial freedom. And, maintaining financial independence within a relationship can foster trust and mutual respect.

Devyani's Journey to Self-Discovery and Independence

Devyani couldn't bear the weight of her emotions any longer. She found the courage to initiate a conversation with Abhay.

Devyani: Abhay, we need to talk.

Abhay looked up from his newspaper, his face unreadable.

Abhay: What's bothering you, Devyani?

Devyani took a deep breath, trying to hold back her tears.

Devyani: Abhay, I feel like I can't breathe in this marriage. You've changed so much since we got married. You were my best friend, and I thought we could handle anything together, but now, it's suffocating.

Abhay frowned, his demeanor turning defensive.

Abhay: Devyani, marriage is different from friendship. I must be the one in charge; that's how it works.

Devyani's heart sank. She had hoped he'd understand.

Devyani: Abhay, I never thought you'd become so controlling. I miss the old you, the one who respected me and valued our opinions equally. Can't we find a middle ground?

Abhay's voice grew stern.

Abhay: Devyani, this is how it is. I won't change my stance on this.

Devyani knew she had to make a difficult decision. She confided in her close friends and even sought the advice of a therapist to understand her situation better.

The therapist explained that Abhay's behavior might indeed be a sign of psychological issues, possibly stemming from insecurity or a need for control. Devyani realized that marrying her best friend might have been a mistake, as the dynamics of a romantic relationship were vastly different from their childhood friendship.

In the end, Devyani decided to prioritize her own happiness and well-being. She sought a respectful and amicable divorce from Abhay, hoping that he would eventually find the help he needed to address his psychological issues. Devyani knew that while marrying a best friend could work for some, it wasn't a guarantee of a successful marriage, and her own happiness and mental health had to come first. It was a heart-wrenching decision, but it was one she felt she had to make to regain her sense of self and find the happiness she had lost.

Breaking Chains

Suvarna had dedicated decades of her life to a marriage that had slowly turned into a nightmare. She endured emotional and physical abuse, all for the sake of her children, Nitisha and Sankalp. Now that her children were settled in their own lives, she felt it was finally time to free herself from this painful relationship.

One evening, Suvarna sat down with her husband, Raman, to have a heart-to-heart conversation. "Raman," she began, her voice trembling with years of pent-up emotions, "I can't continue in this marriage any longer. It's been too much pain, too much suffering."

Raman, a stern man who had never been one to express his emotions, scoffed. "What are you talking about, Suvarna? We've been married for so long, and you want to leave now? What will people say?"

Suvarna's daughter-in-law, Nitisha, had been overhearing the conversation from the next room. She walked in and stood by her mother-in-law's side, her eyes filled with compassion. "Dad, you don't understand the torment Mom has been through all these years. She sacrificed everything for us."

Sankalp, Suvarna's son, chimed in, "Mom, marriage has its ups and downs. It's not always easy. You should try to make it work."

Nitisha couldn't hold back her frustration any longer. "Sankalp, you don't know what Mom has endured for our sake. This isn't just a rough patch; it's been a lifetime of pain."

The tension in the room escalated as Raman's parents joined the conversation. "Suvarna, you've been a terrible wife," Raman's mother said with a scowl. "You're breaking our family apart."

Suvarna's heart ached as she felt the weight of her family's disapproval. But there was one person who stood by her side through it all—her son Arnav. "Mom," he said firmly, "I've seen the pain in your eyes for years. I support your decision, and I'll stand by you no matter what."

Nitisha, unable to bear the hostility any longer, turned to Arnav. "Let's go, Arnav. We don't need to be part of this toxic environment."

Arnav nodded and followed Nitisha out of the house, leaving behind a tumultuous family that was divided over Suvarna's decision.

Days turned into weeks, and Suvarna found solace in the support of her daughter-in-law and son. They helped her navigate the challenging process of ending her marriage and starting a new chapter in her life. Despite the initial chaos, Suvarna finally found the freedom she had yearned for, and with her children by her side, she knew she could face whatever lay ahead.

In the end, Suvarna's story was a testament to the resilience of the human spirit and the strength that comes from the love and support of those who truly understand your pain and stand by your side, no matter what.

Navigating Cultural Barriers and Family Expectations

Once upon a time in a quaint town, there lived Nilay and Nimish, two souls deeply in love. They had known each other since childhood, and their bond had blossomed into a profound love that knew no bounds. However, they were well aware of the cultural and societal barriers that stood in the way of their love.

Solution 1: The Secret Love

Nilay and Nimish decided to keep their love a secret from their families. They met in hidden places, wrote secret love letters, and cherished stolen moments. This clandestine love continued for years, providing them with happiness but also a sense of longing for acceptance.

Solution 2: The Persuasive Approach

Nilay and Nimish decided to confront their families with their love. They believed that if they could eloquently express their feelings and the strength of their relationship, their families might come around. They embarked on a journey to gather support from friends and mentors who could help mediate the conversation with their families.

Solution 3: The Relocation

Realizing the challenges of societal expectations, Nilay and Nimish contemplated moving to a more accepting place where they could live openly as a couple without fear of judgment. They began researching cities and countries that were known for their diverse and inclusive communities.

Solution 4: The Slow Change

Nilay and Nimish decided to focus on changing their families' perceptions over time. They continued their relationship while also working on projects and activities that demonstrated their commitment and love. They hoped that by showcasing their love through their actions, their families would eventually come to accept them.

Solution 5: The Compromise

In a last-ditch effort to gain acceptance from their families, Nilay and Nimish considered compromising on some aspects of their relationship. They knew it wouldn't be easy, but they were willing to make adjustments to honor their families' values while also preserving their love.

As the story unfolds, the paths Nilay and Nimish choose will lead them on different journeys, each filled with its own challenges and triumphs. The ultimate question for them remains: Can love truly conquer all, or will they be forced to make sacrifices for the sake of societal norms and family expectations?

Should they get married as per family wishes and continue their hidden relationship

The decision of whether Nilay and Nimish should get married as per their family's wishes while continuing their hidden relationship is a complex one, and it ultimately depends on their personal values, priorities, and the specific circumstances of their situation. Here are some considerations:

1. Family Expectations: If both Nilay and Nimish highly value family harmony and are willing to make sacrifices for the sake of their families' happiness, getting married as per their families' wishes might seem like a viable option.

2. Long-Term Consequences: They should carefully consider the potential long-term consequences of this decision. Will they be content with a loveless or hidden marriage? Can they sustain this arrangement without causing harm to themselves or their families emotionally?

3. Authenticity: On the other hand, they may feel that living a life that is not true to their authentic selves is emotionally damaging. Continuing a hidden relationship after marriage might lead to feelings of guilt and deceit.

4. Communication: Open and honest communication between Nilay and Nimish is crucial. They need to discuss their feelings, fears, and the impact of such a decision on their mental and emotional well-being.

5. Alternative Solutions: Before making such a significant decision, they could explore alternative solutions, such as seeking support from friends, family, or counselors who may help bridge the gap between their love and their families' expectations.

Ultimately, Nilay and Nimish should carefully weigh the pros and cons of getting married as per their family's wishes while continuing their hidden relationship. They should also consider the impact on their own happiness and well-being.

Love is a powerful force, but it must be balanced with practical considerations and individual values.

Can an overly emotional person change their nature?

It's possible for an emotionally sensitive person to work on managing and regulating their emotions. Emotional intelligence can be developed through self-awareness, self-regulation, and coping strategies. Change may take time and effort, but with practice and potentially with the help of therapy or counseling, individuals can become better at handling their emotions and reactions.

But I feel whenever I tried doing this, I felt claustrophobic.

Changing one's emotional responses and managing emotions can be challenging and might initially feel uncomfortable. It's important to remember that personal growth and change often come with some discomfort. However, it's essential to find strategies and approaches that work for you and seek support if needed. You might consider speaking with a therapist or counselor who can provide guidance and help you navigate this process in a way that feels less overwhelming. Remember, it's okay to seek assistance and take small steps toward managing your emotions.

But is it important for me to change myself?

Whether or not it's important for you to change aspects of yourself, such as your emotional responses, depends on your individual goals, well-being, and how your emotions affect your life and relationships. Change should be a personal choice driven by your own desires for personal growth and improved well-being, rather than external pressure.

If your emotions are causing distress or negatively impacting your life, it might be beneficial to explore ways to manage them better. However, the decision to change should be based on what feels right for you and aligns with your values and goals. It's also important to accept and embrace certain aspects of yourself while working on others, as self-acceptance is a crucial part of personal growth. Consider discussing your feelings and goals with a therapist or counselor who can provide guidance tailored to your specific situation.

I really can't stop getting attached to people and loving them, but ultimately, it's me who is always left alone.

It's natural to form attachments and love people, but it can be challenging when it feels one-sided or leads to feelings of loneliness. It's important to find a balance between forming connections and taking care of your own well-being.

Consider these steps:

1. Self-care: Prioritize self-love and self-care. Focus on activities and practices that bring you joy and fulfillment independently of others.

2. Boundaries: Set healthy boundaries in your relationships. It's okay to give love and care, but ensure it's reciprocated and that you're not overextending yourself.

3. Communication: Talk openly with your loved ones about your feelings and needs. Effective communication can help build stronger, mutually satisfying relationships.

4. Seek support: Reach out to friends, family, or a therapist to discuss your attachment patterns and feelings of loneliness. They can offer valuable insights and support.

5. Independence: Nurture your independence and personal interests. Cultivating a sense of self outside of your relationships can boost your self-esteem and reduce dependence on others for happiness.

Remember that finding the right balance can take time, but it's possible to form healthy and fulfilling relationships while also maintaining your own well-being.

People say as a man it's not right to be over emotional; it's women's trait.

It's important to challenge gender stereotypes and recognize that emotions are a human trait, not limited to any specific gender. Everyone, regardless of their gender, has emotions, and it's healthy to express and manage them.

Society's expectations about gender roles and emotions have evolved over time, and there is a growing understanding that men can and should be able to express their emotions openly. Suppressing emotions or adhering to traditional stereotypes can have negative consequences on mental health.

It's essential to be true to yourself and express your emotions in a way that feels comfortable and authentic to you, irrespective of gender stereotypes. Seeking support, such as talking to a therapist or counselor, can help you navigate these societal pressures and embrace your emotions in a healthy way. Remember, emotional well-being is important for everyone.

I feel I have wasted my whole life caring for others, but still, I do the same.

It's common for people to prioritize caring for others, but it's also essential to ensure that you're taking care of yourself and finding a balance. It's never too late to make changes in your life to prioritize your well-being and personal goals.

Consider the following steps:

1. Self-reflection: Take some time to reflect on your own needs, desires, and goals. What do you want to achieve in your life, and what makes you happy?

2. Set boundaries: Learn to say "no" when necessary and establish healthy boundaries in your relationships to ensure that you're not overextending yourself.

3. Self-care: Make self-care a priority. This includes activities that promote your physical, mental, and emotional well-being.

4. Seek support: Reach out to friends, family, or a therapist who can provide guidance and support as you work towards finding a healthier balance in your life.

5. Gradual changes: You don't have to make drastic changes overnight. Small, gradual steps toward prioritizing yourself can lead to significant improvements over time.

Remember that caring for yourself is not selfish; it's necessary for your own happiness and well-being. By taking steps to find that balance, you can still care for others while also fulfilling your own needs and aspirations.

Friends or family, what's more important?

The importance of friends versus family can vary greatly from person to person and depends on individual circumstances and relationships. Both friends and family play crucial roles in our lives.

Family often provides a strong support system and a sense of belonging, as these relationships are typically long-lasting and deeply rooted. However, not all family relationships are healthy or supportive, so their importance can vary.

Friends can offer companionship, understanding, and a different perspective. Friendships are often based on shared interests and values, and they can be chosen, allowing for a greater degree of compatibility.

Ultimately, what's more important may depend on the quality of the relationships within both your family and friend circles.

Some people find their strongest support from friends, while others have incredibly close and supportive family bonds. What matters most is the quality of the connections and the sense of support and love you receive from those relationships.

Is it important to get married to be committed?

Marriage is one way to formalize commitment, but it's not the only way, nor is it essential for everyone. Commitment can take many forms, and what's most important is that it aligns with your personal values, beliefs, and the preferences of you and your partner (if you're in a relationship).

Some people choose not to marry but are deeply committed to their partners and build successful, long-lasting relationships. Others find marriage to be an important symbol of their commitment. It's a personal choice that varies from person to person and couple to couple.

What's most vital is open and honest communication with your partner about your expectations and desires regarding commitment, whether that includes marriage or not. Respect for each other's views and choices is key in any committed relationship.

1. **Celebrating a Decade of Togetherness:**

Jiya and Jahaan host a surprise anniversary party for themselves, showcasing their unwavering commitment. Their friends witness a genuine bond that has thrived without the confines of a traditional marriage, challenging the notion that commitment is only defined by a legal contract.

2. **Supporting Each Other's Dreams:**

When Jahaan decides to pursue a career change, Jiya stands by him, providing the emotional support and encouragement he needs. Their dynamic challenges the stereotype that only married couples can be pillars of strength for each other.

3. **Navigating Tough Times Together:**

During a challenging period in their lives, Jiya and Jahaan demonstrate resilience and unity. Their ability to face adversity without the label of marriage proves that commitment goes beyond societal expectations, showcasing a deeper connection forged by their hearts.

4. **Co-Parenting Bliss:**

Despite not being married, Jiya and Jahaan seamlessly embrace parenthood. They divide responsibilities, share the joys and challenges, and prioritize their child's well-being. Their harmonious approach challenges the assumption that marriage is a prerequisite for successful parenting.

5. **Spontaneous Adventures:**

The couple takes a spontaneous trip, embracing the freedom that comes with their commitment to each other. Their adventurous spirit defies stereotypes, illustrating that a strong bond doesn't require a marriage certificate but thrives on shared experiences and genuine affection.

6. **Unwavering Trust and Understanding:**

Jiya and Jahaan navigate situations that test their trust and understanding. Their ability to communicate openly and resolve conflicts without the societal pressure of marriage impresses friends and family, proving that commitment stems from mutual respect and love rather than a legal agreement.

Jiya and Jahaan, despite not being married, have seamlessly integrated into each other's families, forming a tight-knit bond that transcends traditional relationships.

One weekend, they decide to organize a surprise family reunion, bringing both their sets of parents, siblings, and extended family together. As the families mingle, it becomes evident that Jiya and Jahaan have cultivated equally strong relationships with each other's kin.

During the gathering, Jiya's mother, having always appreciated Jahaan's respectful and caring demeanor, confides in him about a personal matter. Jahaan listens attentively, offering support and advice just as he would to his own family.

Simultaneously, Jiya finds herself in a heart-to-heart conversation with Jahaan's father. Sharing anecdotes and laughter, they discover common interests and values. Jiya's ability to connect with Jahaan's family reflects her genuine commitment to not only Jahaan but also to the people who hold significance in his life.

Throughout the day, the families witness the mutual respect, warmth, and genuine affection Jiya and Jahaan share with each other's relatives. By the end of the reunion, it becomes evident that their commitment goes beyond just the two of them; it extends to embracing and cherishing each other's families as their own. This situation exemplifies how, despite not being in a conventional marriage, Jiya and Jahaan have fostered bonds that are equally strong with both sets of families.

Why it's important in turbulent relationships not to involve an outsider or society.

A turbulent relationship refers to a partnership characterized by frequent and intense ups and downs, emotional volatility, and instability. In such relationships, conflicts may arise frequently, leading to emotional distress for one or both partners. Turbulence can manifest as arguments, misunderstandings, dramatic emotional shifts, and difficulty in maintaining a sense of stability and harmony. These relationships often lack consistent communication, trust, and a sense of security. Turbulence may be fueled by various factors, including unresolved issues, incompatible communication styles, or external stressors. It's important for individuals in turbulent relationships to seek support, whether through open communication, counseling, or other means, to work towards a healthier and more stable connection.

In turbulent relationships, it's often advisable not to involve outsiders or society for several reasons:

1. Privacy and Trust: Personal relationships are built on trust and intimacy. Involving outsiders can breach this trust and undermine the privacy that couples need to work through their issues.

Malti, grappling with the emotional turmoil of her unstable marriage, sought solace in her close friend Abha. Over late-night conversations and tearful confessions, Malti bared her soul, sharing the intricacies of her struggles, uncertainties, and frustrations with Abha.

Concerned for her friend's well-being, Abha, with good intentions, decided to address the issue directly. She approached Rohan, Malti's husband, and delicately conveyed Malti's feelings, hoping for a constructive dialogue to mend their relationship.

However, Rohan, feeling blindsided and invaded, took Abha's intervention as a breach of privacy. He was upset that Malti had shared their personal matters with someone else, seeing it as a betrayal of the sacred institution of marriage.

A heated confrontation ensued between Rohan and Abha. Misunderstandings escalated, and both parties became entrenched in their perspectives. Despite Abha's sincere intentions to help, Rohan felt cornered and undermined. The conflict grew intense, with accusations and hurtful words exchanged.

In the aftermath, the once-close trio found themselves at an impasse. The rift between Rohan and Abha widened, fueled by hurt feelings and a lack of willingness to understand each other's perspectives. Attempts at reconciliation fell on deaf ears, and they eventually chose to part ways, their friendship irreparably damaged.

The story highlights the delicate balance in navigating the complexities of personal relationships, emphasizing the importance of communication, empathy, and respecting boundaries. In this case, despite good intentions, the fallout led to the dissolution of both Malti's marriage and the friendship between Abha and Rohan.

2. Misinterpretation: Outsiders may not fully understand the complexities of the relationship. They might misinterpret situations, taking sides or offering advice that doesn't fit the context, potentially making things worse.

Raj, a colleague of Shama and Fahad, inadvertently became the source of misunderstanding that cast a shadow over their marital life. One day, during a casual office conversation, Raj overheard snippets of a discussion between Shama and Fahad that seemed strained due to a recent disagreement.

Misinterpreting the situation, Raj jumped to conclusions about the state of Shama and Fahad's marriage. Unaware of the nuances and context of their conversation, Raj began spreading unintentional gossip among their colleagues, inadvertently adding fuel to the fire of misunderstandings.

As the rumors spread, Shama and Fahad started noticing changes in their interactions. Trust eroded, and suspicion crept into their relationship. The misinterpretation by Raj had sown seeds of doubt, leading to tense conversations, miscommunications, and growing resentment between the couple.

Concerned about their marriage, Shama and Fahad eventually confronted each other, attempting to unravel the layers of misunderstanding. It took sincere efforts to bridge the gap created by Raj's unintentional gossip. They realized the need for open communication, sharing their feelings, and understanding each other's perspectives to rebuild the trust that had been damaged.

Recognizing the role played by Raj's misinterpretation, Shama and Fahad decided to address the issue collectively. They approached Raj, explaining the true nature of their disagreement and how the miscommunication had affected their relationship. Raj, remorseful about the unintended consequences of his words, apologized and played a role in clarifying the situation among their colleagues.

With time, patience, and a commitment to rebuilding their relationship, Shama and Fahad managed to overcome the challenges posed by the misinterpretation. The experience strengthened their bond, teaching them the importance of resilience and clear communication in the face of external influences that could potentially strain a relationship.

3. Control and Autonomy: Couples should have control over their own relationship dynamics. Involving outsiders can lead to interference, making it harder for the individuals involved to make their own decisions and find solutions.

4. Stigmatization: Involving society can lead to judgment and stigmatization, which can be harmful to both individuals and

the relationship itself. It may exacerbate feelings of shame or inadequacy.

5. Learning and Growth: Turbulent relationships can provide opportunities for personal growth and learning. When problems are resolved within the relationship, individuals can develop better communication and problem-solving skills.

6. Temporary Nature of Issues: Some relationship issues are temporary and can be worked through. Involving outsiders can escalate minor problems unnecessarily, potentially leading to long-term damage.

However, it's important to note that there are exceptions. If a relationship becomes abusive, harmful, or dangerous, involving outsiders like therapists, counselors, or trusted friends and family members may be necessary for safety and well-being. Each situation is unique, and seeking professional help can be a wise choice when necessary.

The dynamics of a relationship can shift when priorities change. Sometimes your priorities evolve, and sometimes theirs do. This can lead to the fading of love between you and the other person. When you are their top priority, they respond promptly, send long messages, make time for you even when they're busy, and eagerly await your messages or calls. They value your presence, respect your feelings, and understand your silence. Their love and care for you are unwavering.

However, when you are no longer their priority, they may not respond quickly, reply with short messages, ignore you even when free, and become irritated by your attempts to communicate. They only value your presence when they need something from you, respect your feelings only when it aligns with their mood, and understand your silence only when they want to be understood. Their expressions of love and care may become superficial, lacking genuine feeling.

The same can be true for you when your priorities change. Love can fade, and the nature of your bond can shift as priorities evolve over time. This is a common experience in many relationships. It can be painful to realize that you are no longer a significant part of someone's life.

To navigate this situation, remember that in life, people come and go, but life itself continues. Understand that a beautiful life awaits you, so don't dwell on the past. While it's important not to give up easily on your relationships, if someone no longer wants to be with you, it's essential to move on. Moving on doesn't necessarily mean cutting them out of your life; it means not relying on them for your happiness. Treat them as a normal friend without expecting anything in return.

Some people may come into your life to bring happiness, but they might only stay for a short while. Cherish the moments they shared with you, be thankful for the lessons they taught you, and appreciate that they made your life better, even if briefly. Don't blame them for leaving, and don't forget those who continue to stand by your side. Each person who enters your life has a purpose and can teach you valuable lessons. They come and go for a reason.

Certainly, let's delve deeper into these concepts with real-life stories as examples:

1. Trust and Insecurity:

- Story 1 - Emily and John: Emily has experienced past relationships where her partners were unfaithful. These painful memories have left a mark on her mind. Now, she's in a loving relationship with John, who is completely faithful and committed. However, because of her past experiences, Emily's mind frequently generates doubts and insecurities. She may question John's actions, even when there's no reason to doubt him. This constant mistrust, stemming from her past, creates tension in their relationship.

- Story 2 - Michael and Sarah: On the other hand, Michael and Sarah have built a strong foundation of trust. They openly communicate and address any concerns that arise. Sarah's previous relationships were also plagued by mistrust, but she made a conscious effort to overcome her insecurities. Michael's consistent honesty and support have reinforced her newfound trust. Their relationship thrives because they've worked on their individual thought processes.

2. Urge to Cheat and Lie:

- Story 1 - David and Lisa: David is in a committed relationship with Lisa, but he encounters a strong attraction to a colleague at work. His mind begins to rationalize pursuing this attraction, convincing him that it's harmless and exciting. Eventually, he gives in to his desires, resulting in lies and cheating, damaging his relationship with Lisa.

- Story 2 - Alex and Megan: In contrast, Alex also faces a similar attraction outside his relationship with Megan. However, he recognizes these feelings as natural but doesn't let them dictate his actions. He communicates openly with Megan about his struggles and seeks ways to strengthen their bond. His self-awareness and control over his thoughts prevent lies and infidelity, preserving their trust.

3. Love and Anger:

- Story 1 - Sarah and James: Sarah and James have been together for years, but lately, they've been arguing frequently. Sarah's mind tends to magnify minor issues, interpreting them as signs that James doesn't care about her. This leads to escalating arguments and growing resentment, driven by her skewed perceptions.

- Story 2 - Maria and Carlos: Maria and Carlos have also faced challenges in their relationship, but they approach them differently. They acknowledge that misunderstandings can happen and don't rush to conclusions. Instead of letting anger control their interactions, they engage in calm, empathetic communication. Their relationship benefits from their ability to manage their thoughts and emotions.

In each of these stories, the role of our thoughts and mindset in shaping relationships is evident. Trust issues, infidelity, love, and anger all stem from how individuals perceive and respond to their own thoughts and emotions. By recognizing the power of their minds and working on self-awareness and communication, couples like Michael and Sarah and Alex and Megan can build stronger, healthier relationships, while others may face challenges like Emily and John or David and Lisa when their thoughts aren't managed effectively.

Get into a relationship only when you are absolutely okay not being in a relationship"

Certainly! The advice "Get into a relationship only when you are absolutely okay not being in a relationship" may seem counterintuitive at first, but it underscores a crucial aspect of healthy relationships. A truly healthy relationship is one where both individuals are content and fulfilled on their own, without relying on the relationship to fill a void or address personal dissatisfaction.

When you actively seek a relationship primarily because of personal dissatisfaction or a sense of need, it can lead to an unhealthy dynamic. In such cases, the relationship is often burdened with unrealistic expectations, as one or both individuals may look to the other to solve their problems or make them happy. This can create pressure and strain on the relationship.

A strong and fulfilling relationship, on the other hand, occurs when both individuals are already content and whole as individuals. In this scenario, they come together not out of desperation or need but because they genuinely enhance each other's lives. Each person adds value to the other's life, rather than relying on the relationship to provide something they lack. This leads to a synergy where the partnership becomes greater than the sum of its individual parts.

We all go throught this

You find someone attractive, and they're equally interested in you, so you decide to enter a relationship. However, over time, you realize it's not working out, leading to a breakup. During the post-breakup phase, people often express their feelings with sad quotes and engage in some form of online stalking, essentially wasting their time.

One observation in life is that relationships that start quickly tend to end just as swiftly. So, the advice is to take things slowly. Go on dates, spend time together, and truly get to know each other. These dates don't need to be extravagant; sometimes, simple moments like sharing coffee on a couch can work wonders. The key is to engage in meaningful conversations and reflect on why you love the other person – is it genuine affection or mere infatuation?

Enjoy the journey of getting to know each other, as the destination, a beautiful relationship, will come naturally. Love is a journey where two imperfect individuals walk together, striving for perfection. Only commit to a relationship when you're certain of your feelings. And remember, if a relationship doesn't work out, don't tarnish the beauty of love because of one experience. Keep loving and keep growing in love.

Would you allow someone else to choose your underwear or advise you on which ones to discard?

Most likely not.

Underwear is a personal and private matter, much like a romantic relationship. Only you can truly understand how it fits and feels. Just as poorly fitting underwear can be uncomfortable, external advice on your relationship may not always apply.

In a romantic relationship, it's a unique and personal connection between you and your partner. While friends may offer advice, remember that it's ultimately your love story. Instead of letting others interfere, appreciate and cherish your relationship, much like you would with a classy pair of underwear.

Avoid relying too heavily on friends' advice, as it can sometimes lead to misunderstandings. Everyone's relationships are different, just as each person's fingerprint is unique. Your friends might not have the same experiences or insights into your relationship. So, while you can listen to their input, trust your own judgment and follow your heart, because it's your love story, not theirs.

The dynamics of a relationship can shift when priorities change. Sometimes your priorities evolve, and sometimes theirs do. This can lead to the fading of love between you and the other person. When you are their top priority, they respond promptly, send long messages, make time for you even when they're busy, and eagerly await your messages or calls. They value your presence, respect your feelings, and understand your silence. Their love and care for you are unwavering.

However, when you are no longer their priority, they may not respond quickly, reply with short messages, ignore you even when free, and become irritated by your attempts to communicate. They only value your presence when they need something from you, respect your feelings only when it aligns with their mood, and understand your silence only when they want to be understood. Their expressions of love and care may become superficial, lacking genuine feeling.

The same can be true for you when your priorities change. Love can fade, and the nature of your bond can shift as priorities evolve over time. This is a common experience in many relationships. It can be painful to realize that you are no longer a significant part of someone's life.

To navigate this situation, remember that in life, people come and go, but life itself continues. Understand that a beautiful life awaits you, so don't dwell on the past. While it's important not to give up easily on your relationships, if someone no longer wants to be with you, it's essential to move on. Moving on doesn't necessarily mean cutting them out of your life; it means not relying on them for your happiness. Treat them as a normal friend without expecting anything in return.

Some people may come into your life to bring happiness, but they might only stay for a short while. Cherish the moments they shared with you, be thankful for the lessons they taught you, and appreciate that they made your life better, even if briefly. Don't blame them for leaving, and don't forget those who continue to stand by your side. Each person who enters your life has a purpose and can teach you valuable lessons. They come and go for a reason.

Real and Fake Relationship

Distinguishing between a real and fake relationship can be challenging, but here are some key factors to consider:

1. Communication: In a real relationship, there is open and honest communication. Both partners are willing to listen, share their thoughts, and work through issues together. In a fake relationship, communication may be shallow or filled with lies.

2. Emotional Connection: Genuine relationships are built on a deep emotional connection. Partners care about each other's well-being and support each other through ups and downs. In fake relationships, this emotional connection is often lacking or superficial.

3. Consistency: Real relationships endure over time, with both partners consistently showing love, care, and commitment. In fake relationships, there may be inconsistency or a lack of effort to maintain the connection.

4. Trust: Trust is a cornerstone of real relationships. In fake ones, trust may be repeatedly broken or never established in the first place.

5. Shared Values and Goals: Real relationships often involve shared values, interests, and long-term goals. In fake relationships, these elements may be absent or forced.

6. Intimacy: Real relationships involve physical and emotional intimacy that goes beyond surface-level interactions. In fake relationships, intimacy may be missing or used manipulatively.

7. Respect: Mutual respect is a key component of real relationships. In fake ones, disrespect or manipulation may be more prevalent.

8. Independence: In real relationships, both partners maintain their individuality while sharing their lives. In fake relationships, one partner may try to control or change the other.

9. Transparency: Real relationships involve transparency and a willingness to share personal information. Fake relationships may involve secrecy or a lack of disclosure.

10. Supportive Network: Real relationships often have the support and approval of friends and family, while fake relationships may raise concerns among loved ones.

Remember that it's not always easy to distinguish between real and fake relationships, and sometimes it takes time and reflection to make a clear assessment. Trust your instincts and seek advice from trusted friends or a counselor if you have doubts about a relationship.

Romantic relationships are diverse and can take many forms, each with its own dynamics and characteristics. Here are some common types of romantic relationships:

1. Monogamous Relationship: This is the most traditional form of a romantic relationship, where two individuals exclusively commit to each other. They focus on building a deep emotional connection and often aspire to create a long-term partnership.

2. Open Relationship: In an open relationship, partners agree that they can have romantic or sexual interactions with others outside the primary partnership. Communication and clear boundaries are crucial to make this type of relationship work.

3. Polyamorous Relationship: Polyamory involves engaging in multiple romantic or sexual relationships simultaneously, with the knowledge and consent of all involved parties. Trust,

honesty, and effective communication are essential in polyamorous relationships.

4. Long-Distance Relationship: When partners live far apart, they maintain their romantic connection through communication and occasional visits. Trust and effective communication are vital in making long-distance relationships function.

5. Casual Dating: Some people prefer to keep things light and non-committal, engaging in casual dating where they enjoy each other's company without the expectation of a serious relationship. These relationships can be short-term or evolve into something more.

6. Same-Sex Relationship: These are romantic relationships between individuals of the same gender. They function similarly to heterosexual relationships but may face unique challenges related to societal acceptance and legal recognition.

7. Age-Gap Relationship: Partners in these relationships have a significant difference in age. Managing generational gaps and expectations can be a key factor in making these relationships work.

8. Interracial or Interethnic Relationship: These relationships involve individuals from different racial or ethnic backgrounds. Cultural understanding, respect, and communication are crucial to navigate potential cultural differences.

9. Arranged Marriage: In some cultures, marriages are arranged by families, and the couple may not know each other well before marriage. These relationships rely on mutual respect and a willingness to adapt and grow together.

10. LGBTQ+ Relationships: These encompass a range of relationships among LGBTQ+ individuals. While they

function similarly to heterosexual relationships, they may involve additional challenges related to discrimination and social acceptance.

In all types of romantic relationships, communication, trust, and mutual respect are foundational. The specific dynamics and functions of a relationship depend on the individuals involved, their goals, and their unique circumstances. Successful romantic relationships often require effort, compromise, and a willingness to grow and adapt together.

Why open relationships are not acceptable by society

Societal acceptance of open relationships varies greatly across cultures, communities, and individuals. It's important to recognize that attitudes toward open relationships are not universally negative, and opinions on this matter can be highly subjective. However, there are several reasons why some people or societies may be less accepting of open relationships:

1. Traditional Values: Many societies have deeply ingrained traditional values that prioritize monogamy as the ideal form of a romantic relationship. These values can be influenced by religious beliefs, cultural norms, and historical practices.

2. Jealousy and Insecurity: Open relationships often challenge the notions of exclusivity and can trigger feelings of jealousy and insecurity in some individuals. This discomfort can lead to negative perceptions of open relationships.

3. Fear of Relationship Instability: Some people believe that open relationships are less stable and more likely to lead to emotional turmoil or breakup. The idea of having multiple partners can be seen as a potential source of instability.

4. Lack of Understanding: Open relationships can be misunderstood or misrepresented in media and popular

culture. This lack of understanding can contribute to negative stereotypes and misconceptions.

5. Social Stigma: Open relationships can face social stigma and discrimination. People in open relationships may fear judgment or discrimination from family, friends, or colleagues, which can discourage them from being open about their relationship choices.

6. Legal and Financial Complexities: In some places, legal and financial structures are primarily designed for monogamous couples, which can create challenges for those in open relationships when it comes to issues like inheritance, healthcare, or child custody.

7. Moral or Religious Beliefs: Some individuals or communities have strong moral or religious objections to non-monogamous relationships, considering them sinful or immoral.

How does polyamorous relationships function, can a couple be happy and contented in this relationship also

Polyamorous relationships can function well when all parties involved communicate openly, honestly, and consent to the arrangement. In polyamory, individuals have multiple romantic or sexual relationships simultaneously, with the knowledge and consent of all involved parties. Here's how they typically function and some factors that can contribute to happiness and contentment:

1. Communication: Effective communication is paramount in polyamorous relationships. All partners must discuss their needs, boundaries, and expectations regularly. Honest and clear communication helps build trust and maintain a healthy balance among multiple relationships.

2. Consent: Everyone involved in a polyamorous relationship should willingly and enthusiastically consent to the arrangement. Consent ensures that all parties are comfortable with the dynamics and can make informed decisions.

3. Boundaries: Establishing and respecting boundaries is crucial. Partners in polyamorous relationships should have a clear understanding of what is acceptable behavior within the relationship and what is not. Boundaries help prevent misunderstandings and conflicts.

4. Emotional Management: Managing emotions can be more complex in polyamorous relationships due to multiple connections. Partners must be emotionally mature and supportive, handling jealousy, insecurity, and other feelings in a healthy manner.

5. Time Management: Balancing time among multiple partners can be challenging. Successful polyamorous relationships require good time management and prioritization

to ensure that each partner feels valued and appreciated.

6. Trust and Honesty: Trust is the foundation of any relationship, and it's even more critical in polyamory. Being honest about feelings, desires, and other relationships is essential to maintain trust.

7. Compersion: Compersion is the positive feeling one experiences when witnessing their partner's happiness with someone else. Cultivating compersion rather than jealousy can lead to greater happiness in polyamorous relationships.

8. Community and Support: Some people find it helpful to connect with like-minded individuals in the polyamorous community for advice, support, and understanding.

As for happiness and contentment, polyamorous relationships can indeed lead to fulfillment for those who choose this lifestyle. Many people in polyamorous relationships report feeling a deeper sense of personal growth, expanded emotional connections, and enhanced communication skills. However, it's important to note that polyamory is not suitable for everyone, and not all individuals or couples may find happiness in this type of arrangement.

The key is to be self-aware, communicate openly, and prioritize the well-being of all involved. Some individuals and couples are very content and fulfilled in polyamorous relationships, while others may prefer monogamy. Ultimately, the success and happiness in any type of relationship depend on the compatibility, values, and communication skills of the individuals involved.

It's important to note that these reasons for societal non-acceptance are not universal, and attitudes toward open relationships are evolving in many places. Open relationships are a valid choice for consenting adults who communicate openly and honestly about their desires and boundaries. Ultimately, societal acceptance or rejection of open relationships is a complex and culturally specific issue that continues to evolve over time.

Is casual dating perfect for healthy romantic relationships

Casual dating can be a valid and enjoyable way to engage in romantic relationships, but whether it's "perfect" for healthy romantic relationships depends on individual preferences, goals, and circumstances. Here are some considerations:

Pros of Casual Dating for Healthy Relationships:

1. Low Pressure: Casual dating allows individuals to enjoy the company of others without the immediate pressure of long-

term commitment. It can be a low-stress way to get to know different people.

2. Exploration: It provides an opportunity to explore different personalities and dating experiences, helping individuals gain a better understanding of their own preferences and needs in a partner.

3. Independence: Casual dating often allows for greater personal independence and freedom, as there are typically fewer expectations and obligations compared to more serious relationships.

4. Focus on Self-Growth: It can be a time for self-discovery and self-growth, as individuals have the freedom to prioritize personal development and pursue their interests.

5. Flexibility: Casual dating can be adaptable to changing life circumstances, making it suitable for people who have busy or uncertain schedules.

Cons of Casual Dating for Healthy Relationships:

1. Emotional Complexity: Casual dating can become emotionally complex, as feelings may develop over time, leading to confusion or heartache if both partners are not on the same page.

2. Lack of Commitment: Some individuals may find that casual dating lacks the emotional depth and security they desire in a long-term relationship.

3. Misaligned Expectations: If one person is looking for a committed relationship while the other is only interested in casual dating, it can lead to disappointment and conflict.

4. Risk of Miscommunication: Clear communication is essential in casual dating to avoid misunderstandings or unintentional hurt feelings.

5. Social Stigma: In some cultures or communities, casual dating may be stigmatized or not well-accepted.

Whether casual dating is perfect for a healthy romantic relationship depends on the individuals involved and their mutual understanding. It can be a great fit for those who prioritize personal freedom and exploration or for individuals who are not ready for a committed relationship at a particular stage in their lives.

However, it's essential that all parties involved are on the same page regarding their expectations and intentions to ensure that the casual dating experience remains positive and respectful. Open and honest communication is key to navigating the complexities of casual dating and maintaining healthy relationships, whether they are casual or long-term commitments.

How does heterosexual and same-sex relationship same How romance can be missing in heterosexual relationship but not in same-sex relationships

Heterosexual and same-sex relationships share many similarities, as both involve romantic and emotional connections between individuals. Love, affection, and the desire for emotional intimacy are universal aspects of human relationships that can be present in both heterosexual and same-sex couples. However, there are also unique experiences and challenges associated with each type of relationship.

Common Elements in Both Heterosexual and Same-Sex Relationships:

1. Emotional Connection: Both types of relationships can involve a deep emotional connection, where partners care for and support each other.

2. Romantic Love: Romantic feelings, attraction, and love can be present in both heterosexual and same-sex couples.

3. Intimacy: Emotional and physical intimacy are important in both types of relationships, contributing to the sense of closeness and connection.

4. Commitment: Many heterosexual and same-sex couples commit to long-term partnerships, which can involve shared goals, living arrangements, and responsibilities.

5. Challenges: Both types of relationships can face challenges such as communication issues, conflicts, and external pressures.

Differences in the Experience of Romance:

The idea that romance may be missing in a heterosexual relationship but not in a same-sex relationship is a subjective notion that varies greatly among individuals and couples. It's important to avoid making sweeping generalizations, as the presence or absence of romance is not determined by sexual orientation but rather by individual personalities, preferences, and relationship dynamics. Some key points to consider:

1. Individual Differences: The presence or absence of romance is highly individual. Some heterosexual couples may have intensely romantic relationships, while others may not prioritize or express romance in the same way.

2. Relationship Dynamics: Romance can manifest differently in various relationships. Some couples express their love through romantic gestures, while others emphasize other forms of connection, such as shared interests, humor, or emotional support.

3. External Factors: External factors, such as stress, work-life balance, or health issues, can affect the perception of romance in any relationship, regardless of sexual orientation.

4. Cultural and Societal Influences: Cultural and societal norms can influence how people express and perceive romance, but these norms can vary widely between cultures and change over time.

Ultimately, the presence or absence of romance in a relationship is a complex and personal matter that depends on the individuals involved, their unique dynamics, and their preferences. It's essential to avoid making assumptions about the nature of any relationship based solely on sexual orientation, as love and connection can be found in all types of partnerships.

How successful age gap romantic relationship

The success of an age-gap romantic relationship depends on various factors, and there is no one-size-fits-all answer. Age-gap relationships can be successful and fulfilling for many couples, but they also come with unique challenges that need to be navigated effectively. Here are some factors to consider:

1. Communication: Effective communication is crucial in any relationship, but it becomes even more essential in age-gap relationships. Open and honest discussions about expectations, life goals, and concerns are key to building a strong foundation.

2. Shared Values and Goals: Partners should share common values and have compatible life goals, or they should be willing to compromise and find ways to harmonize their aspirations despite the age difference.

3. Emotional Connection: A strong emotional connection is essential for relationship success. Both partners should feel loved, respected, and emotionally fulfilled in the relationship.

4. Respect and Equality: Age-gap relationships should be built on mutual respect and equality. Neither partner should feel inferior or superior due to age.

5. Supportive Social Circles: The support of friends and family can significantly impact the success of an age-gap relationship. Acceptance and understanding from loved ones can make it easier to overcome challenges.

6. Handling Life Stages: Partners may be at different life stages due to the age difference. It's important to discuss and plan for how to handle issues like retirement, family planning, and career changes.

7. Coping with Age-Related Differences: Age-gap couples may face challenges related to differences in energy levels, interests, and health. Open discussions and adaptability are key to addressing these issues.

8. Legal and Financial Considerations: Be aware of legal and financial implications, such as inheritance, retirement, and healthcare, that can be affected by the age gap.

It's worth noting that many age-gap relationships are successful and happy. Age differences, while significant, do not necessarily determine the quality or longevity of a relationship. Compatibility, emotional connection, and a willingness to work through challenges are far more critical factors.

Ultimately, the success of an age-gap relationship depends on the individuals involved and how well they communicate, understand, and support each other. If both partners are committed to making the relationship work and are willing to address any issues that arise due to the age gap, there's a good chance of building a healthy and fulfilling partnership.

Why people try to hide problems in their relationships

People often try to hide problems in their relationships for various reasons:

1. Fear of judgment: They may worry that others will judge them or their partner negatively if they reveal their relationship problems.

2. Protecting their image: People may want to maintain a positive image in front of friends, family, or on social media, so they hide issues to avoid appearing vulnerable or flawed.

3. Fear of confrontation: Addressing problems can be uncomfortable and may lead to arguments or difficult conversations, which some individuals want to avoid.

4. Hope for resolution: Some people believe that the issues will resolve themselves over time, so they wait before discussing them openly.

5. Cultural or societal norms: Cultural or societal expectations may discourage discussing relationship problems openly, leading individuals to keep their issues private.

6. Preserving the relationship: In some cases, people hide problems in an attempt to preserve the relationship and avoid causing additional stress or hurt to their partner.

7. Lack of communication skills: Some individuals may not know how to effectively communicate their concerns and emotions, leading them to keep problems hidden.

It's important to remember that hiding problems in a relationship can often make them worse. Open and honest communication is typically a healthier way to address issues and work towards solutions.

Is it advisable to continue with toxic relationships just cause of peer pressure?

No, it is not advisable to continue with a toxic relationship solely because of peer pressure or external influences. Your well-being and mental health should always be a top priority. Toxic relationships can be emotionally, mentally, and even physically harmful. Staying in such a relationship can lead to long-term negative consequences.

It's important to make decisions about your relationships based on your own feelings, values, and what's best for you, rather than succumbing to peer pressure. Seek support and advice from trusted friends and family members who have your best interests at heart, but ultimately, the decision should be yours.

If you find yourself in a toxic relationship, it's often recommended to seek professional help or counselling to better understand the situation and explore options for improving it or, if necessary, safely ending the relationship. Your mental and emotional well-being should always be a priority.

What exactly is toxic relationship, how to make sure you are in a toxic relationship?

A toxic relationship is characterized by harmful, negative, and unhealthy patterns of behaviour, communication, and interactions between two people. These relationships can have a detrimental impact on one's emotional, mental, and sometimes physical well-being. Here are some signs to help you recognize if you might be in a toxic relationship:

1. **Constant Negativity: ** In a toxic relationship, negativity is pervasive. There may be frequent arguments, criticism, and

blame, with little to no positive or constructive communication.

Nikita, a vibrant and ambitious young woman, found herself entangled in a toxic relationship with Naman. Despite her initial optimism, Naman's constant negativity cast a shadow over their connection. His critical comments and pessimistic outlook began to erode Nikita's self-esteem and enthusiasm.

As days turned into months, Nikita struggled to maintain her sense of identity and happiness. Naman's controlling behavior isolated her from friends and family, leaving her feeling trapped in a cycle of negativity. Despite the toxicity, she hesitated to break free, torn between the love she once felt and the toll it took on her well-being.

One day, as Nikita reflected on her situation, she realized the need for change. Summoning courage, she confronted Naman about the toxic dynamics of their relationship, expressing her desire for positivity and growth. The conversation was difficult, emotions ran high, but it marked a pivotal moment.

With a heavy heart, Nikita chose to prioritize her mental and emotional health. She distanced herself from Naman, seeking support from loved ones and professional guidance. Breaking free from the toxic bond, Nikita embarked on a journey of self-discovery and healing, determined to rebuild her life on a foundation of positivity and self-love.

2. **Control and Manipulation: ** One partner may exert control or manipulate the other's thoughts, actions, or decisions. This can involve emotional manipulation, guilt-tripping, or coercive behaviour.

In the small town of Serenity, Nandini's life took an unexpected turn. Entrapped in a toxic relationship with Aditya, his manipulative control eroded Nandini's self-confidence. One day, overwhelmed by despair, she contemplated ending her life.

However, fate intervened in the form of Riya, Nandini's close friend. Sensing something amiss, Riya reached out to her, offering a listening ear and unwavering support. Recognizing the severity of the situation, Riya decided to take Nandini to a counselor.

With the counselor's guidance, Nandini began to unravel the layers of manipulation and control that had bound her for so long. Slowly, she regained her strength and rediscovered her worth. Through therapy sessions and the support of friends, Nandini started rebuilding her life.

She severed ties with Aditya, surrounded herself with positive influences, and focused on self-love. Nandini's journey of healing became an inspiration to others facing similar challenges. Her story spread through the town, fostering awareness about the importance of mental health and the resilience of the human spirit.

In time, Nandini not only overcame her past but also became an advocate for mental health, helping others break free from the chains of toxic relationships. Her transformation showcased the power of friendship, professional help, and inner strength in rebuilding a shattered life.

3. **Lack of Trust: ** Trust is essential in any healthy relationship. In a toxic one, trust may be consistently broken, and suspicions or jealousy may be common.

4. **Isolation: ** Toxic partners may try to isolate you from friends and family, making you dependent on them for emotional support and companionship.

Raman consistently criticizes Rama's friends and family, planting seeds of doubt about their intentions. He manipulates her into thinking they are not trustworthy, subtly isolating her from her support network.

Raman imposes strict rules on Rama's activities, constantly monitoring her whereabouts and demanding detailed explanations for her every move. This control tactic creates a sense of isolation and dependence on him for approval.

Raman subtly undermines Rama's self-esteem by making derogatory comments about her abilities and appearance. This emotional manipulation erodes her confidence, making her hesitant to seek validation or support from anyone else.

Raman uses gaslighting techniques, making Rama doubt her own perceptions and memories. By distorting reality and convincing her that her concerns are unfounded, he isolates her from a clear understanding of the unhealthy dynamics in their relationship, trapping her in a cycle of self-doubt.

What is gaslighting technique in relationship

Gaslighting is a form of psychological manipulation where one person seeks to sow seeds of doubt in another, making them question their perception, memory, or sanity. In toxic relationships, it can be used to gain control and undermine the victim's confidence. Examples include denying events that occurred, trivializing the other person's feelings, or accusing them of being overly sensitive or paranoid. Over time, gaslighting can lead to self-doubt and confusion in the victim.

5. **Verbal or Physical Abuse: ** This is a clear sign of a toxic relationship. If there is any form of verbal or physical abuse, it's crucial to seek help and support to leave the situation safely.

6. **Constant Drama: ** Toxic relationships often involve a lot of drama and instability. The relationship feels like a rollercoaster with extreme highs and lows.

Jealousy Unleashed:

Arnav innocently mentions a new colleague, leading Maya to explode in a fit of jealousy. Accusations fly, and Maya confronts the colleague at Arnav's workplace, causing a scene that leaves everyone bewildered.

Social Media Meltdown:

Maya stumbles upon an innocent comment on Arnav's social media, misinterprets it, and decides to publicly shame Arnav online. This escalates into a heated argument, involving friends and family, turning a simple misunderstanding into a full-blown digital battleground.

The Misunderstood Gift:

Arnav excitedly presents Maya with a thoughtful gift, but Maya interprets it as an insult. This triggers an emotional confrontation where Arnav finds himself defending his intentions, only to be met with Maya's unwarranted anger and an escalating exchange that leaves both emotionally drained.

Isolation Tactics:

Arnav plans a night out with friends to lift Maya's spirits, but she accuses him of neglecting her. Maya retaliates by manipulating situations to isolate Arnav from his support system, causing tension and strain in his friendships as he struggles to balance his relationship with Maya and maintain connections with his friends.

7. **Lack of Respect: ** Respect is a fundamental element of a healthy relationship. In a toxic one, respect for boundaries, individuality, and personal space is frequently disregarded.

8. **Feeling Drained: ** If you constantly feel emotionally drained, anxious, or unhappy in the relationship, it may be toxic.

9. **No Personal Growth: ** Healthy relationships should support personal growth and self-improvement. In toxic relationships, personal growth may be stifled or discouraged.

10. **Repeated Pattern: ** If you notice a pattern of these negative behaviours recurring over time, it's a strong indicator of a toxic relationship.

If you suspect you are in a toxic relationship, it's essential to prioritize your well-being and consider seeking help from a therapist, counsellor, or a trusted friend or family member. Ending a toxic relationship can be challenging, but it's often necessary for your long-term happiness and mental health.

How to explain your partner that the relationship is over from your side without any hard feelings. When you person on other end really love you .

Simran: (Nervously) Ranjan, can we talk about something important?

Ranjan: (Concerned) Of course, Simran. What's on your mind?

Simran: (Deep breath) Well, you know how much I care about you, and this isn't easy for me to say, but I think it's time we end our relationship.

Ranjan: (Surprised) Wait, what? Simran, is something wrong? Did I do something to upset you?

Simran: (Quickly) No, Ranjan, you've been amazing, and you haven't done anything wrong. It's just that, over time, I've realized that my feelings have changed, and I can't ignore them anymore.

Ranjan: (Saddened) I see. So, you don't love me anymore?

Simran: (Softly) It's not that I don't care about you, Ranjan. It's just that I don't feel the same way I used to, and I think it's only fair to both of us that we end things now, rather than dragging it out.

Ranjan: (Nods) I appreciate your honesty, Simran. It hurts, but I'd rather you be honest with me than keep something like this hidden.

Simran: (Tears welling up) Ranjan, please know that I'm so sorry for this situation. You're an incredible person, and you deserve someone who can love you the way you deserve to be loved.

Ranjan: (Takes a deep breath) Thank you, Simran, for being honest with me, even if it's painful. I don't want us to harbor any hard feelings towards each other. We had some beautiful moments together.

Simran: (Wipes away tears) Yes, we did. I'll always cherish those moments, and I hope we can part on good terms, as friends.

Ranjan: (Nods) I hope so too, Simran. Let's give each other the space we need to heal and move forward separately.

Simran: (Sighs with relief) Thank you for understanding, Ranjan. You've been so kind about all of this.

Ranjan: (Smiles softly) I want you to be happy, Simran, even if it means we have to go our separate ways. Take care of yourself.

Simran: (With a shaky smile) You too, Ranjan. I'll always wish you the best.

If Ranjan takes the news of the breakup hard and is struggling with his mental and emotional well-being, it's essential to approach the situation with care and empathy. Here are some steps both Simran and Ranjan can consider:

For Simran:

1. Offer Support: Simran should be understanding and empathetic toward Ranjan's feelings. She can let him know that she cares about his well-being and is there to support him as a friend.

2. Give Space: While it's crucial to offer support, Simran should also respect Ranjan's need for space if he requests it. Everyone copes with breakups differently, and some individuals may need time alone to process their emotions.

3. Encourage Self-Care: Simran can suggest and encourage self-care activities that may help Ranjan cope with his emotions, such as talking to a therapist or counselor, engaging in hobbies, and spending time with friends and family.

For Ranjan:

1. Seek Support: Ranjan should not hesitate to reach out to friends, family, or a mental health professional for support and guidance. Talking to someone can provide valuable emotional support and coping strategies.

2. Allow Time to Grieve: It's normal to feel a sense of loss after a breakup, and Ranjan should allow himself to grieve the end of the relationship. This process may take time, but it's essential for healing.

3. Focus on Self-Improvement: This period of transition can be an opportunity for personal growth and self-improvement. Ranjan can use this time to set new goals and work on himself.

4. Avoid Isolation: While it's okay to spend some time alone, isolating oneself for an extended period can be detrimental.

Ranjan should try to maintain connections with friends and engage in social activities when he feels ready.

Both Simran and Ranjan should remember that healing from a breakup is a process that takes time, and it's okay to seek professional help if the emotional distress becomes overwhelming. It's crucial for both parties to prioritize their mental and emotional well-being during this challenging time.

Is simran right in taking this decision

Simran's decision to end the relationship, even though her boyfriend Ranjan still loves her, is a personal one, and it can be considered the right decision for several reasons:

1. **Honesty**: Simran is being honest with herself and with Ranjan about her changing feelings. In any relationship, honesty is crucial. It's better to address these feelings early on rather than pretending or leading someone on.

2. **Respecting Her Feelings**: Simran acknowledges that her feelings have changed over time. Feelings are not always under our control, and it's important to respect one's emotions. She recognizes that continuing the relationship when her heart isn't fully in it wouldn't be fair to Ranjan.

3. **Avoiding Unnecessary Pain**: By ending the relationship now, Simran is preventing both herself and Ranjan from potential future heartache. Continuing a relationship when one person's feelings have changed can lead to resentment, unhappiness, and hurt feelings.

4. **Valuing the Relationship**: Simran values the relationship they had by acknowledging its importance and choosing to part on amicable terms. By ending it respectfully, she is leaving the door open for a potential friendship down the road.

5. **Self-Care**: Simran is taking care of her own emotional well-being. In a healthy relationship, both individuals should prioritize their happiness and mental health. If Simran believes that continuing the relationship would lead to her feeling unfulfilled or unhappy, it's essential for her to prioritize her own well-being.

It's important to note that relationships are complex, and every situation is unique. Simran's decision may be right for her given her circumstances and feelings. However, it's equally important for Ranjan to respect her decision and prioritize his own emotional well-being as well. In the end, open communication and respect for each other's feelings are key to handling such situations as gracefully as possible.

How gender roles can impact family dynamics

Gender roles can significantly impact family dynamics by shaping the expectations and behaviors of individuals within a family. Let's illustrate this with an example involving Shraddha and Shravan:

Shraddha and Shravan are a married couple in a traditional society where gender roles are well-defined. In this context:

1. **Division of Labor**: Gender roles often dictate specific roles within the family. For instance, Shravan is expected to be the primary breadwinner, while Shraddha is expected to take on the role of a homemaker. This division of labor can lead to a power imbalance within the family, with Shravan making most of the financial decisions and Shraddha taking care of household chores and child-rearing.

2. **Decision-Making**: Because of the traditional gender roles, Shravan may assume that he has the final say in important family decisions, especially those related to finances or major life choices. This can lead to a lack of autonomy for

Shraddha, and her opinions and desires may not be given equal consideration.

3. **Emotional Expression**: Gender roles can also influence how emotions are expressed within the family. Shravan may feel societal pressure to suppress his emotions, particularly those considered "soft" or vulnerable. Shraddha, on the other hand, may be encouraged to express her emotions more freely, which can lead to potential misunderstandings between them.

4. **Parenting Styles**: Gender roles can extend to parenting styles. Shraddha may be expected to be the nurturing and caring parent, while Shravan may be expected to be the disciplinarian. This can result in differences in how they interact with their children and can affect the children's perception of gender roles as they grow up.

5. **Career Aspirations**: Gender roles can impact career choices and opportunities. Shravan might feel pressured to pursue a high-paying but demanding job to fulfill his role as the primary provider, potentially sacrificing work-life balance. Meanwhile, Shraddha's career ambitions may be limited due to societal expectations of her primary role as a homemaker.

Overall, gender roles can create expectations and norms that influence how Shraddha and Shravan interact within their family. These roles can lead to unequal power dynamics, limited individual fulfillment, and potential conflicts if either of them desires a different role or wants to challenge these traditional expectations. It's important for families to have open and respectful communication to address and adapt to these dynamics in a way that works for everyone involved.

Minal and Naman, born and raised in the picturesque town of Jabalpur, had always cherished the simplicity of their hometown. The quiet streets, the familiar faces, and the rich culture were ingrained in their hearts. Yet, they were well aware of the opportunities that awaited their children, Nitya and Nimish, in far-off lands.

As Nitya pursued her dreams in Canada, studying engineering at a prestigious university, Nimish ventured to New Zealand to explore his passion for environmental science. Although the geographical distance seemed vast, the bond within their family remained unbreakable, thanks to modern technology. Video calls and instant messaging brought them together, bridging the miles that separated them.

Minal and Naman had a profound understanding of their children's ambitions and aspirations. They didn't want their kids to be tethered to their hometown, even if it meant staying apart. The parents were proud of Nitya and Nimish's accomplishments and supported them wholeheartedly. They believed in the importance of growth and the pursuit of one's dreams, just as they had once dreamed for themselves.

The kids, in return, were deeply respectful of their parents' wishes. They knew that Minal and Naman had sacrificed much to provide them with a good education and ample opportunities. They promised to stay closely connected, sharing their lives through screens and occasionally making the long journey back home.

Over the years, Nitya and Nimish excelled in their respective fields. Nitya became an accomplished engineer working on cutting-edge technology, and Nimish became an environmentalist making strides in sustainability. Despite the physical distance, the siblings continued to be each other's pillars of support, often brainstorming and sharing ideas across continents.

As time passed, Minal and Naman gracefully embraced the quietude of their hometown. They took solace in the knowledge that their children were flourishing. Their bond with Nitya and Nimish grew stronger through virtual connections, and they eagerly awaited their visits.

The grandchildren arrived eventually, bringing an extra layer of warmth and joy to the family. The kids, too, became adept at navigating technology to keep in touch with their grandparents. They would chat, share school stories, and celebrate birthdays together, albeit through screens.

Minal and Naman, despite their initial reservations about leaving Jabalpur, found solace in the knowledge that their decision had allowed their children to soar. The geographical distance never severed their familial ties, thanks to the wonders of modern technology. In this tale of love, support, and the pursuit of dreams, the family proved that no matter the physical separation, their hearts remained eternally connected.

Once upon a time in the heart of Jodhpur, Rajasthan, there lived Thakur Ranjeet Singh, a respected patriarch of his family and a shrewd businessman. Ranjeet Singh was known far and wide for his entrepreneurial prowess and his deep connection to the land of kings.

Ranjeet Singh had four younger brothers: Veerendra, Rajat, Harish, and Vikram. Each brother had his unique talents and strengths. Veerendra was a skilled horseman, Rajat a savvy trader, Harish a talented craftsman, and Vikram an astute accountant. Together, they formed a formidable team.

The Singh family had always been deeply rooted in their ancestral land, which they cultivated and turned into thriving farmlands and orchards. However, Ranjeet Singh saw the winds of change blowing, and he knew they had to diversify. So, with the support of his brothers, they ventured into various businesses – from textiles to trading spices.

As the businesses grew, so did the extended family. Nieces, nephews, cousins, and in-laws all found their place within the Singh dynasty. This close-knit network provided a strong sense of belonging and security to everyone. The family rallied around each other in times of joy and sorrow, ensuring no member was ever left in the lurch.

But amidst this sense of unity, power dynamics began to take root. Ranjeet Singh was the natural leader, given his age and experience. His decisions often carried the most weight, leading to some resentment among his younger brothers, who felt their contributions were undervalued.

This power struggle wasn't limited to the brothers alone; it trickled down to the next generation. The cousins, who had grown up together, found themselves competing for recognition and influence within the family empire. Family gatherings became less about celebration and more about subtle maneuvers and positioning.

Despite the underlying tension, the Singh family's businesses continued to thrive. Their combined efforts and diverse skill sets allowed them to weather economic storms and emerge even stronger. Their strong bonds of kinship and shared history kept them together, even when disagreements threatened to tear them apart.

It was during a heated family meeting one evening, when tensions had reached their peak, that Ranjeet Singh proposed a radical idea. He suggested that they formally divide the businesses among the brothers, granting each autonomy over their respective ventures. This way, he hoped to alleviate the power struggles and allow each brother to shine in his own right.

Reluctantly, the brothers agreed to the plan. Over time, they nurtured their individual enterprises, and the Singh family continued to prosper. The cousins too, found their paths, collaborating and competing in a healthy and productive manner.

In the end, Ranjeet Singh's decision not only preserved their family's unity but also allowed each member to grow independently. The power dynamics that once threatened to consume them were channelled into healthy competition, propelling the Singh family and their businesses to new heights, while the bonds of kinship remained as strong as ever. The legacy of Thakur Ranjeet Singh and his brothers continued to flourish, reminding them all that, in the end, it was family that mattered most.

Theoretical Perspectives on Relationship

Attachment theory, developed by John Bowlby and further expanded by Mary Ainsworth, is a psychological framework that explains how early relationships between infants and their caregivers can shape their emotional and social development. It suggests that the quality of these early attachments can have long-lasting effects on a person's relationships and emotional well-being throughout their life.

Let's use examples of three different pairs to illustrate attachment styles:

1. Ratna and Mithun:

- Ratna is a responsive and emotionally available caregiver. She consistently meets Mithun's emotional and physical needs, providing comfort and support.

- Mithun, in this secure attachment style, trusts Ratna to be there when he needs her. He explores the world confidently, knowing he has a secure base to return to.

- This secure attachment is likely to lead to Mithun developing healthy relationships and good emotional regulation skills.

2. Manjay and Rohini:

- Manjay is inconsistent in responding to Rohini's needs. Sometimes he's attentive and caring, but at other times, he's distant or neglectful.

- Rohini develops an anxious-ambivalent attachment style. She becomes clingy and anxious, never sure if Manjay will be there for her.

- As an adult, Rohini may have difficulty trusting her partners and may be overly concerned about the stability of her relationships.

3. Nilay and Nimish:

- Nilay is largely unresponsive to Nimish's needs. He rarely engages with Nimish emotionally, and his caregiving is neglectful.

- Nimish develops an avoidant attachment style. He learns to self-soothe and becomes emotionally distant from Nilay to protect himself from disappointment.

- In adulthood, Nimish may struggle with intimacy and find it challenging to open up emotionally to romantic partners.

Attachment theory helps us understand how early caregiving experiences can shape our emotional and relational tendencies. Keep in mind that attachment styles are not fixed; they can evolve and change through therapeutic interventions and life experiences.

What is Social Exchange Theory. How it effects relationships

Social exchange theory is a sociological and psychological concept that seeks to explain how individuals evaluate and make decisions about their relationships, including friendships, romantic partnerships, and even business relationships. It is based on the idea that human interactions are fundamentally transactions where individuals seek to maximize their rewards and minimize their costs.

Key components of social exchange theory include:

1. Rewards: These are the positive experiences, benefits, or outcomes that individuals gain from being in a relationship.

Rewards can include emotional support, companionship, financial assistance, or any other form of gratification.

2. Costs: Costs are the negative aspects or sacrifices associated with a relationship. These can include time and effort invested, compromises made, or any discomfort or inconvenience experienced in the relationship.

3. Comparison Level (CL): Individuals have a comparison level, which represents their expectations of what they should receive from a relationship based on past experiences or societal norms. If the rewards exceed this comparison level, they are more likely to view the relationship positively.

4. Comparison Level for Alternatives (CLalt): This is the assessment of available alternatives to the current relationship. If individuals perceive that they can find a better relationship elsewhere, they may be less committed to their current one.

The effects of social exchange theory on relationships can be summarized as follows:

1. Relationship Satisfaction: According to the theory, individuals are most satisfied in relationships where the rewards outweigh the costs and where their expectations (CL) are met or exceeded. When this balance is achieved, people tend to be more content in their relationships.

2. Commitment: The theory suggests that commitment to a relationship is influenced by the perception of alternatives. If individuals believe there are better alternatives available (high CLalt), they may be less committed to their current relationship.

3. Decision-Making: Social exchange theory can explain decision-making in relationships. People may choose to enter, maintain, or exit a relationship based on their assessment of the rewards, costs, and alternatives.

4. Long-Term Outcomes: Over time, the evaluation of rewards and costs in a relationship can impact its longevity. If the balance is consistently negative, individuals may be more likely to end the relationship.

It's important to note that social exchange theory is just one perspective on relationships, and human relationships are complex and influenced by many factors, including emotions, values, and cultural norms. While the theory provides valuable insights into how individuals assess and manage their relationships, it doesn't capture the full richness of human interactions and emotions.

Interdependence theory detailed explanation needed

Interdependence theory is a social psychology and relationship theory that focuses on how individuals in relationships make decisions and interact with one another based on their perceptions of interdependence. Developed by social psychologists Harold Kelley and John Thibaut, this theory is particularly relevant in understanding how individuals in various types of relationships, such as friendships, romantic partnerships, or business collaborations, navigate their interactions.

Here's a detailed explanation of the key components of interdependence theory:

1. **Interdependence:** At the core of this theory is the concept of interdependence, which refers to the extent to which individuals rely on each other to achieve their goals or meet their needs. Interdependence can range from low to high, depending on how much each person's outcomes (rewards or costs) are influenced by the actions and choices of the other person in the relationship.

2. **Outcomes:** Outcomes in interdependence theory are the results or consequences that individuals experience as a result of their actions and the actions of their partner in the relationship. These outcomes can be positive (rewards) or negative (costs). Rewards can include things like emotional support, companionship, or financial benefits, while costs might involve sacrifices, compromises, or emotional distress.

3. **Comparison Levels (CL):** Each individual in a relationship has a personal Comparison Level (CL), which is a standard or reference point representing their expectations about what they should receive from the relationship. It is influenced by past experiences, societal norms, and personal values. If an individual's outcomes in the relationship meet or exceed their CL, they are likely to be satisfied and committed to the relationship.

4. **Comparison Level for Alternatives (CLalt):** The Comparison Level for Alternatives (CLalt) is the assessment of what an individual believes they could achieve in an alternative relationship or situation. If an individual perceives that they could have better outcomes in an alternative scenario, they may be less satisfied and committed to their current relationship.

5. **Decision-Making:** Interdependence theory is often used to understand how individuals make decisions in relationships. People consider their own outcomes, their partner's outcomes, their CL, and their CLalt when deciding whether to stay in a relationship, invest more in it, or exit and seek an alternative.

6. **Types of Interdependence:**

- **Positive Interdependence:** When individuals perceive that their outcomes are positively influenced by their partner's actions, they are more likely to cooperate and invest in the relationship.

- **Negative Interdependence:** In contrast, when individuals perceive that their outcomes are negatively impacted by their partner's actions, they may compete or seek alternatives.

Interdependence theory helps explain how individuals navigate the complexities of social and personal relationships by considering the balance between their expectations, their perceived alternatives, and the actual outcomes they experience. It has been influential in fields such as social psychology, communication studies, and relationship counseling, providing insights into how people manage and sustain their relationships.

Communication theory in relationships

Communication theory plays a crucial role in understanding and improving relationships. Effective communication is a cornerstone of healthy, successful relationships, whether they are romantic, familial, professional, or friendships. Here are several communication theories applied to relationships:

1. **Social Exchange Theory:** In the context of relationships, social exchange theory suggests that individuals assess the costs and rewards associated with being in a particular relationship. Successful relationships often involve a balance where both partners perceive a fair exchange of benefits and contributions.

- **Example:** In a romantic relationship, partners may evaluate whether the emotional support, companionship, and shared experiences (rewards) outweigh the effort, compromises, and occasional disagreements (costs) they invest in the relationship.

2. **Communication Accommodation Theory:** This theory emphasizes how individuals adjust their communication styles to match or adapt to their relationship partners. Effective communication often involves accommodating differences in communication styles to enhance understanding and rapport.

- **Example:** Imagine two partners in a relationship: one prefers direct and explicit communication, while the other is more indirect and subtle. To communicate effectively, they may need to accommodate each other's styles to prevent misunderstandings.

3. **Attachment Theory:** Attachment theory, originally developed by John Bowlby and expanded by Mary Ainsworth, explores how early attachment experiences with caregivers influence adult relationships. It highlights the importance of emotional responsiveness and support in fostering secure attachments in adult relationships.

- **Example:** A person with a secure attachment style tends to have trust and confidence in their partner's emotional availability. They are more likely to express their needs and emotions openly, leading to better communication and relationship satisfaction.

4. **Relational Dialectics Theory:** This theory suggests that relationships are dynamic and involve ongoing tensions or dialectics between opposing desires or needs. Effective communication involves acknowledging and managing these tensions.

- **Example:** In a long-distance relationship, there may be a dialectic between the desire for independence and the need for closeness. Effective communication involves discussing and finding a balance between spending time apart and maintaining connection.

5. **Gottman's Four Horsemen:** Developed by relationship researcher John Gottman, the "Four Horsemen of the Apocalypse" are communication patterns that predict relationship distress. They include criticism, contempt, defensiveness, and stonewalling. Recognizing and addressing these patterns is vital for maintaining healthy relationships.

- **Example:** If one partner habitually criticizes the other's actions or decisions, it can lead to defensiveness and resentment. Effective communication involves expressing concerns or frustrations without resorting to criticism or contemptuous language.

6. **Interpersonal Communication Skills:** Effective communication in relationships often requires mastering essential skills such as active listening, empathy, assertiveness, and conflict resolution. These skills enhance understanding and promote constructive interactions.

- **Example:** When a conflict arises in a relationship, active listening and empathy can help partners better understand each other's perspectives and work together to find mutually satisfying solutions.

These communication theories provide valuable insights into how people can foster healthier and more satisfying relationships by understanding communication dynamics, addressing challenges, and nurturing positive interactions. Effective communication is at the heart of building and maintaining strong, lasting connections with others.

How to build and maintain healthy relationships

Building and maintaining healthy relationships involves various factors, including communication, trust, respect, and empathy. Here are some key tips:

1. Effective Communication:

- Listen actively to understand the other person's perspective.

- Express your thoughts and feelings honestly and respectfully.

- Use "I" statements to express your emotions and needs.

2. Trust:

- Be reliable and consistent in your actions.

- Keep promises and avoid betraying the other person's trust.

- Trust is built over time; give it time to develop.

3. Respect:

- Treat each other with kindness and consideration.

- Respect boundaries and personal space.

- Value each other's opinions and differences.

4. Empathy:

- Try to understand and share the other person's feelings.

- Offer support during challenging times.

- Show compassion and care.

5. Conflict Resolution:

- Address conflicts calmly and constructively.

- Focus on the issue, not the person.

- Seek compromise and find solutions together.

6. Quality Time:

- Spend meaningful time together.

- Create shared experiences and memories.

- Balance individual and shared interests.

7. Independence:

- Maintain your individual identities and interests.

- Avoid becoming overly dependent on each other.

- Encourage personal growth and self-care.

8. Apologize and Forgive:

- Be willing to apologize when you make mistakes.

- Forgive and let go of past grievances.

- Holding onto grudges can harm a relationship.

9. Boundaries:

- Establish clear boundaries to define what's acceptable.

- Communicate boundaries openly and respect each other's limits.

- Boundaries help maintain a healthy balance.

10. Seek Help When Needed:

- If issues persist, consider couples counseling or therapy.

- Professional guidance can provide valuable insights and strategies.

Remember, building and maintaining healthy relationships is an ongoing process that requires effort from both parties. Open and honest communication is often the key to resolving issues and fostering a strong, lasting connection.

How important is trust and honesty in a relationship

Trust and honesty are fundamental cornerstones of a healthy and successful relationship. Here's why they are crucial:

1. Trust:

- Trust forms the foundation of any meaningful relationship. Without trust, it's challenging to build a strong connection.

- It creates a sense of safety and security within the relationship, allowing individuals to be vulnerable and open with each other.

- Trust is essential for emotional intimacy, as it enables people to share their thoughts, feelings, and fears without fear of betrayal.

- Healthy trust means having confidence in your partner's reliability, faithfulness, and integrity.

2. Honesty:

- Honesty is closely linked to trust. Being truthful and transparent builds and reinforces trust over time.

- It promotes clear and effective communication within the relationship, preventing misunderstandings and deception.

- Honesty fosters a sense of authenticity and genuineness between partners, which is essential for a deep and meaningful connection.

- It helps resolve conflicts and address issues openly, leading to healthier problem-solving and relationship growth.

In summary, trust and honesty are essential because they create a solid and secure emotional foundation for a relationship. When both partners can trust each other and be honest in their interactions, the relationship is more likely to thrive, as it allows for genuine connection, emotional intimacy, and effective conflict resolution. Without these qualities, a relationship can become strained and less fulfilling.

In situations where telling the truth might jeopardize a relationship, it's important to consider the context and the potential consequences carefully. Here are some steps Ranjan can consider:

1. Reflect on the Situation:

- Take time to think about the situation and its implications.

- Consider the importance of the truth versus the potential impact on the relationship.

2. Weigh the Pros and Cons:

- Assess the potential outcomes of both telling the truth and not telling the truth.

- Consider whether there are alternative ways to address the issue without compromising honesty.

3. Seek Advice:

- Talk to trusted friends, family members, or a counselor to gain different perspectives on the situation.

- They may offer valuable insights and guidance.

4. Communicate Tactfully:

- If Ranjan decides not to disclose certain information, he should still aim for open and honest communication on other matters.

- Avoid lying or being deceptive, but focus on other aspects of their relationship.

5. Evaluate the Long-Term:

- Think about the long-term prospects of the relationship. Is it sustainable if honesty is compromised continuously?

- Consider whether the relationship aligns with both partners' values and needs.

6. Reassess Over Time:

- As circumstances change or evolve, Ranjan and Nikita may need to revisit the issue and decide if it's appropriate to disclose the truth later.

Ultimately, the decision to tell the truth or withhold information should be made carefully, taking into account the unique dynamics of the relationship and the individuals involved. Ranjan should prioritize his own values and well-being while also being sensitive to Nikita's perspective and background. If the situation allows, open and honest communication is generally the best approach, but there may be instances where discretion is necessary to protect the relationship or avoid harm.

What if both partners lack communication skills and always end up fighting when ever they start talking about a issue

If both partners in a relationship lack communication skills and frequently end up in fights when discussing issues, it's important to work together to improve communication. Here's a step-by-step approach to address this issue:

1. **Acknowledge the Problem:**

- Both partners should recognize that there is an issue with communication and a pattern of arguments.

2. **Take a Break When Necessary:**

- If discussions escalate into fights, it's okay to take a break and cool down before returning to the conversation. Agree on a signal or word to use when one of you needs a break.

3. **Seek Professional Help:**

- Consider couples counseling or therapy with a trained therapist who can provide guidance and teach effective communication skills.

4. **Practice Active Listening:**

- Learn to actively listen to each other without interrupting. Show empathy and understanding when your partner is speaking.

5. **Use "I" Statements:**

- Express your thoughts and feelings using "I" statements to avoid blaming or accusing each other. For example, say, "I feel hurt when..." instead of "You always..."

6. **Stay Calm and Respectful:**

- Keep your emotions in check during conversations. Avoid shouting, name-calling, or becoming defensive.

7. **Focus on Solutions, Not Blame:**

- Shift the focus of discussions toward finding solutions rather than assigning blame. What can you both do to resolve the issue?

8. **Set Ground Rules:**

- Establish ground rules for communication, such as no yelling, no interrupting, and taking turns speaking.

9. **Practice Outside of Conflicts:**

- Work on communication skills during everyday conversations, not just when conflicts arise.

10. **Be Patient:**

- Improving communication takes time and effort. Be patient with each other's progress and setbacks.

11. **Celebrate Progress:**

- Acknowledge and celebrate small improvements in your communication. Positive reinforcement can motivate both partners.

Remember that building better communication skills is an ongoing process. It's important for both partners to be committed to making these improvements for the sake of the relationship. Professional guidance can be particularly valuable in helping couples break destructive communication patterns and build healthier ways of interacting.

Empathy and understanding play pivotal roles in nurturing healthy and harmonious relationships. Let's explore how these qualities can benefit two couples: Soniya and Saaransh, and Sandhya and Kumar.

Soniya and Saaransh:

Soniya has been working long hours recently, and Saaransh has been feeling neglected.

1. **Empathy**: Saaransh practices empathy by trying to understand Soniya's perspective. He realizes that she's been under immense work-related stress lately.

- Instead of accusing her of neglecting him, Saaransh approaches Soniya with empathy, saying, "I can see that work has been really tough for you lately, and I understand that you've had to put in extra hours."

2. **Understanding**: Soniya appreciates Saaransh's understanding. She responds by explaining the challenges at work and how it's affecting her.

- This understanding opens up a conversation where they both express their feelings and concerns. They work together to find a solution that balances their needs and responsibilities.

Sandhya and Kumar:

Kumar feels hurt because Sandhya forgot their anniversary.

1. **Empathy**: Sandhya practices empathy by putting herself in Kumar's shoes. She imagines how she would feel if the situation were reversed.

- Sandhya approaches Kumar with empathy, saying, "I can understand how hurtful it must be for you that I forgot our anniversary. I'm sorry."

2. **Understanding**: Kumar appreciates Sandhya's understanding. He opens up about why their anniversary is meaningful to him and how he felt overlooked.

- Sandhya listens actively and understands the importance of this event for Kumar. She acknowledges her mistake and makes an effort to make it up to him.

In both scenarios, empathy and understanding help the couples navigate challenging situations. Instead of reacting defensively or placing blame, they connect emotionally and strive to comprehend each other's feelings. This fosters a sense of trust and closeness, ultimately strengthening their relationships.

Empathy allows individuals to connect on a deeper level by acknowledging and validating each other's emotions, while understanding encourages open and constructive communication. These qualities are essential for building strong and resilient relationships.

What is conflict resolution in relationship and why it is important

Conflict resolution in a relationship refers to the process of addressing and resolving disagreements, disputes, or conflicts that may arise between partners. It involves finding a peaceful and mutually satisfactory solution to the issue at hand. Conflict resolution is important in relationships for several reasons:

1. **Improved Communication:** Conflict resolution promotes open and effective communication between

partners. It encourages them to express their thoughts, feelings, and concerns in a healthy and respectful manner.

2. **Prevents Escalation:** Unresolved conflicts can escalate and lead to more significant issues and resentment. Addressing conflicts early helps prevent this escalation.

3. **Maintains Emotional Connection:** Handling conflicts constructively can preserve the emotional bond between partners. When conflicts are resolved, it reaffirms the commitment and love in the relationship.

4. **Builds Trust:** Successfully resolving conflicts builds trust between partners. It demonstrates that both individuals are willing to work together to overcome challenges.

5. **Enhances Problem-Solving Skills:** Conflict resolution involves finding solutions to problems. Over time, partners can become more skilled at addressing and solving issues together.

6. **Reduces Stress:** Ongoing conflicts can lead to chronic stress, which can be detrimental to physical and emotional well-being. Resolving conflicts reduces stress levels in the relationship.

7. **Fosters Growth:** Handling conflicts provides opportunities for personal and relationship growth. It allows partners to better understand each other's perspectives and needs.

8. **Promotes Fairness:** Conflict resolution ensures that both partners have a say in the outcome, promoting fairness and equality in the relationship.

9. **Strengthens the Relationship:** Successfully navigating conflicts and finding solutions together can strengthen the relationship's resilience and longevity.

Effective conflict resolution involves active listening, empathy, compromise, and a commitment to finding win-win solutions. It's about addressing the issue at hand while also considering the needs and feelings of both partners. Ultimately, conflict resolution is an essential skill for maintaining healthy and thriving relationships, as it allows couples to overcome challenges and grow together.

Can conflicts be resolved after years of separation, can relationships be back to normal after years of separation

Reconnecting and resolving conflicts after years of separation can be challenging, but it is possible depending on various factors:

1. **Mutual Willingness:** Both parties must be willing to engage in the process of reconciliation and conflict resolution. If one or both individuals are not open to it, it becomes much more difficult.

2. **Communication:** Effective and open communication is crucial. Both individuals need to be able to express their thoughts, feelings, and concerns honestly and respectfully.

3. **Forgiveness:** Forgiveness is often a significant part of reconciling after separation. This includes forgiving each other for past mistakes and moving forward with a clean slate.

4. **Changes and Growth:** People can change and grow over time. If both individuals have evolved positively during the separation, it can increase the chances of a successful reconciliation.

5. **Counseling or Mediation:** Sometimes, professional help in the form of couples counseling or mediation can be beneficial in navigating the process of reconnecting and resolving conflicts.

6. **Realistic Expectations:** It's important to have realistic expectations. The relationship may not return to exactly how it was before the separation, but it can evolve into something new and potentially better.

7. **Time and Patience:** Reconnecting and resolving conflicts may take time. It's important to be patient and allow the process to unfold naturally.

It's worth noting that not all relationships can or should be reconciled. In some cases, the reasons for the separation are insurmountable, and trying to rebuild the relationship may not be in the best interest of either party. It's essential to carefully assess the circumstances and consider what's healthiest for both individuals.

Ultimately, whether a relationship can be back to "normal" or not after years of separation depends on the unique dynamics, willingness, and efforts of the individuals involved. Reconciliation and conflict resolution are possible, but they require time, effort, and a shared commitment to rebuilding the relationship.

Sometimes, it's better not to resolve conflicts after years of separation when major misunderstandings have driven a deep wedge between individuals. Let's consider the example of Nishant and Anshul to understand why:

Nishant and Anshul:

Nishant and Anshul were once close friends who had a falling out due to a significant misunderstanding. Nishant felt that Anshul had betrayed his trust in a critical situation, and Anshul believed that Nishant had misinterpreted his actions. The disagreement led to a heated argument, and they decided to part ways, ending their friendship.

Here's why it might be better for them not to resolve the conflict after years of separation:

1. **Irreparable Trust Issues:** The misunderstanding between Nishant and Anshul was so profound that it resulted in a severe breach of trust. Even after years, the hurt and mistrust may still linger. Attempting to reconcile could mean reopening old wounds and reigniting negative emotions.

2. **Changed Circumstances:** Over the years, Nishant and Anshul have likely evolved, and their lives have taken different paths. Attempting to resolve the conflict might not align with their current priorities and lifestyles.

3. **New Relationships and Support Systems:** During the separation, both Nishant and Anshul may have formed new relationships and support systems. Rekindling their old friendship could potentially disrupt these newer, stable connections.

4. **Closure Through Acceptance:** Sometimes, accepting that a relationship has run its course and moving forward separately can provide closure. In some cases, the effort required to rebuild a broken relationship may outweigh the benefits.

5. **Emotional Well-Being:** Attempting to resolve a deep-seated conflict may bring up painful memories and emotions, potentially impacting their emotional well-being.

In situations like this, it might be more advisable for Nishant and Anshul to acknowledge that their friendship has changed and that it's healthier for both of them to move on independently. Not all conflicts can or should be resolved, especially when they are accompanied by profound misunderstandings and trust issues that may be better left in the past. It's essential for individuals to prioritize their own well-being and personal growth.

relationship stressors as challenge in relationship .

Relationship stressors are external or internal factors that can create challenges in a romantic relationship. They can strain the connection between partners and, if not managed well, may lead to conflicts or even the deterioration of the relationship. Let's explore this concept using an example involving Nisha and Sankalp:

Nisha and Sankalp have been in a committed relationship for several years. They love each other deeply, but they have been facing some relationship stressors that are putting a strain on their bond. Here are a few examples of relationship stressors they are dealing with:

1. **Communication Issues:** Nisha and Sankalp have different communication styles. Nisha prefers to talk openly about her feelings and concerns, while Sankalp tends to be more reserved and finds it challenging to express his emotions. This difference in communication styles can lead to misunderstandings and frustration.

2. **Work-Related Stress:** Sankalp has a demanding job that often requires long hours and frequent business trips. This leads to him being physically and emotionally exhausted, leaving less time and energy for their relationship. Nisha feels neglected and unimportant due to his work commitments.

3. **Financial Strain:** Nisha and Sankalp are struggling with financial issues. They have different spending habits and financial goals, which often leads to arguments about money management. This financial stress is affecting their overall happiness and causing tension in their relationship.

4. **Family Expectations:** Both Nisha and Sankalp come from culturally diverse backgrounds, and their families have certain expectations regarding their relationship, such as marriage and religious practices. Balancing these expectations with their own desires and values can create conflict and stress.

5. **Trust Issues:** In the past, there have been instances of mistrust in their relationship due to misunderstandings and jealousy. Rebuilding trust and addressing these issues is an ongoing challenge for them.

To overcome these relationship stressors, Nisha and Sankalp must engage in open and honest communication, work on understanding and respecting each other's perspectives, seek compromise on financial matters, and set boundaries with their families while maintaining their own values and goals. It's important for them to remember that every relationship faces challenges, and how they navigate these stressors can ultimately strengthen their bond if approached with patience, empathy, and a willingness to work together.

Can a relationship survive without trust and honesty.

Trust and honesty are fundamental pillars of a healthy and sustainable relationship. While relationships can exist without trust and honesty, they are unlikely to thrive in the long term. Let's explore this with examples involving two couples: Prem and Sunayana, and Nishant and Devyani.

Prem and Sunayana:

No, a Relationship Can't Survive Without Trust and Honesty:

Prem and Sunayana have been together for years, but over time, they have developed trust issues. Prem often tells white lies to avoid conflict, while Sunayana has caught him in these lies multiple times. This lack of honesty erodes trust between them. Sunayana, in response, starts hiding her true feelings because she fears Prem's reaction. This further compound the problem, creating a cycle of dishonesty and mistrust. They constantly doubt each other's words and actions, which leads to arguments and insecurity. Over time, their relationship becomes toxic and emotionally draining. Without trust and honesty, they find it nearly impossible to maintain a healthy, loving connection.

Nishant and Devyani:

Yes, a Relationship Can Survive Without Trust and Honesty:

Nishant and Devyani have been together for a while and have faced their fair share of challenges. They have trust issues stemming from past infidelity. However, they decide to seek therapy to address their problems. With professional guidance, they learn to communicate openly and honestly about their feelings, fears, and past mistakes. Nishant admits his infidelity, and Devyani acknowledges her own shortcomings in the relationship. Through therapy and their commitment to rebuilding trust, they manage to mend their bond. They establish new boundaries, rebuild honesty, and gradually regain each other's trust. While it's a challenging journey, their relationship survives because they actively work on rebuilding trust and honesty.

End Results:

- For Prem and Sunayana, the lack of trust and honesty ultimately leads to the breakdown of their relationship. They may either separate or continue in a dysfunctional and unhappy partnership, causing emotional pain for both.

- For Nishant and Devyani, their relationship can survive and even thrive if they are committed to rebuilding trust and honesty. Their journey will require ongoing effort, but it is possible for them to repair their bond and enjoy a healthier, more trusting connection.

In summary, while a relationship can technically exist without trust and honesty, its quality and longevity are severely compromised. Without these essential elements, the relationship is likely to become toxic and unsustainable. Rebuilding trust and honesty through open communication and therapy, as demonstrated by Nishant and Devyani, offers a more promising path to a healthy and lasting partnership.

How jealousy and insecurities kill a relationship

Jealousy and insecurities can have a profoundly negative impact on a relationship, often leading to significant problems and, in extreme cases, the end of the relationship. Let's examine how these emotions can harm a relationship using the example of Nitya and Utkarsh.

Nitya and Utkarsh:

Nitya and Utkarsh have been in a loving relationship for a few years. However, Nitya struggles with jealousy and insecurities. Here's how these emotions can spoil their relationship:

1. **Distrust:** Nitya often becomes suspicious of Utkarsh's interactions with others, especially with people of the opposite gender. Her constant questioning and suspicion make Utkarsh feel as though she doesn't trust him. This erodes the foundation of trust in their relationship.

2. **Frequent Arguments:** Nitya's insecurities lead to frequent arguments and conflicts. She becomes upset if Utkarsh spends time with friends or co-workers, and these arguments disrupt their peace and harmony. The constant tension takes a toll on both emotionally.

3. **Emotional Drain:** Utkarsh feels emotionally drained by Nitya's jealousy and insecurities. He becomes hesitant to share his experiences or even express himself honestly, fearing that it will trigger another argument or make Nitya feel threatened.

4. **Isolation:** Over time, Nitya's jealousy may cause Utkarsh to withdraw from social activities and friendships to avoid conflict. This isolation can be harmful to both partners, as they lose connections outside of the relationship.

5. **Self-Esteem Issues:** Nitya's insecurities can also affect Utkarsh's self-esteem. He may start to feel guilty for simply living his life and being social, which can lead to resentment and dissatisfaction in the relationship.

To what extent do they spoil relationships:

Jealousy and insecurities can spoil a relationship to a significant extent, and the impact can vary depending on the individuals and the degree of these emotions. In many cases, if left unaddressed, they can lead to:

- **Breakdown of Trust:** Trust is a fundamental element of a healthy relationship. Jealousy and insecurities can erode this trust, making it difficult for partners to believe in each other and feel secure.

- **Constant Conflict:** Frequent arguments and conflicts can become exhausting, making the relationship a source of stress rather than comfort.

- **Emotional Distress:** Both partners may experience emotional distress, anxiety, and unhappiness due to the constant negativity in the relationship.

- **Isolation:** One or both partners may isolate themselves from friends and family, which can lead to social and emotional isolation.

- **Ultimately, Breakup:** In extreme cases, the strain caused by jealousy and insecurities can lead to the breakup of the relationship as one or both partners may decide that the constant turmoil is not worth enduring.

It's essential for couples like Nitya and Utkarsh to address these issues through open communication, trust-building exercises, and possibly seeking professional help, such as couples' therapy. Otherwise, jealousy and insecurities can have a lasting and damaging impact on a relationship.

Breakup and divorce are indeed significant challenges in relationships, and they can leave lasting emotional scars. Let's explore the experiences of two couples, Kavya and Kavita, and Srikant and Sunanda, to understand how these events can impact individuals and their lives.

Kavya and Kavita were in a same-sex relationship for several years. Over time, they grew apart, and communication issues and differing life goals strained their bond. Eventually, they decided to break up. Here's how it affected them:

- Emotional Trauma: The breakup was emotionally traumatic for both Kavya and Kavita. They had shared their lives, dreams, and experiences, and the separation felt like a profound loss.

- Loss of Identity: After the breakup, both had to adjust to life as individuals again. This meant redefining their identities outside of the relationship, which can be a challenging process.

- Emotional Scars: The breakup left emotional scars, causing trust issues and making it harder for them to open up in future relationships. They carried the pain and heartbreak with them for a long time.

- Growth and Healing: Over time, Kavya and Kavita focused on personal growth and healing. While the scars remained, they learned valuable lessons about themselves and what they wanted from future relationships.

Srikant and Sunanda were married for a decade before deciding to get a divorce due to irreconcilable differences. Their experiences highlight the challenges of divorce:

- Legal and Financial Implications: Divorce often involves legal and financial complexities, such as dividing assets and determining alimony and child custody arrangements. This process can be stressful and emotionally draining.

- Impact on Children: Srikant and Sunanda had children, and the divorce had a profound impact on them. Coping with the changes in family dynamics was emotionally challenging for all involved.

- Social Stigma: In some cultures, divorce can carry a social stigma, leading to feelings of shame or isolation. Srikant and Sunanda had to navigate these societal pressures.

- Rebuilding Lives: After the divorce, both had to rebuild their lives separately. This included finding new homes, jobs, and support networks, which can be overwhelming.

- Emotional Healing: Divorce can leave emotional scars, affecting self-esteem and future relationships. Srikant and Sunanda underwent therapy to heal and move forward with their lives.

In both cases, breakup and divorce presented significant challenges and left lasting scars. However, with time, self-reflection, and support, individuals can heal and even grow stronger. These experiences can provide valuable life lessons and help individuals make better choices in future relationships. While the scars may remain, they don't have to define one's future happiness and fulfillment.

Avoiding a breakup or divorce when a relationship has deteriorated significantly isn't always the best idea. In some cases, staying in a relationship that has become toxic or unbearable can be detrimental to the well-being of both individuals involved. Here are some considerations:

1. Mental and Emotional Health: Continuing in a relationship that has deteriorated to the point of causing mental and emotional distress can be harmful. Prolonged unhappiness, anxiety, and stress can have serious consequences for one's mental health.

2. Physical Health: Chronic stress from a troubled relationship can also impact physical health. It can lead to issues like insomnia, high blood pressure, and other stress-related health problems.

3. Quality of Life: Staying in a dysfunctional relationship can negatively affect one's overall quality of life. It can limit personal growth, happiness, and fulfillment.

4. Impact on Children: If there are children involved, witnessing a toxic relationship can be harmful to them as well. It may be better for their well-being if their parents separate and provide a healthier environment.

5. Individual Growth: Sometimes, ending a relationship that isn't working allows individuals to focus on personal growth, self-discovery, and finding happiness independently.

However, it's essential to approach the decision to end a relationship or pursue a divorce thoughtfully and considerately. Here are some steps to consider:

1. Communication: Try to communicate openly and honestly with your partner about your concerns and feelings. Sometimes, issues can be resolved through improved communication.

2. Counseling or Therapy: Consider couples' counseling or individual therapy to work through relationship challenges and explore whether there's potential for improvement.

3. Assess the Future: Reflect on whether the relationship has any realistic chance of getting better or if it's genuinely irreparable.

4. Legal and Financial Considerations: In the case of marriage, consult with legal professionals to understand the implications of divorce, especially concerning assets, child custody, and alimony.

5. Support Network: Lean on your support network, such as friends and family, for guidance and emotional support during this challenging time.

Ultimately, the decision to avoid or pursue a breakup or divorce should prioritize the well-being and happiness of the individuals involved. In many cases, ending a relationship that is causing pain and unhappiness can be the healthier choice, allowing both individuals to move forward and find greater fulfillment in their lives.

Embracing Insight

As we gracefully traverse the concluding chapter of "Little Secrets of Relationships," let us delve into the profound value of gaining an outsider's perspective on our emotional journey. Relationships, intricate and multifaceted, often find us deeply entrenched in our convictions, believing we hold the key to righteousness.

Take a reflective pause to step outside the confines of your emotional cocoon and behold your relationship through the lens of a compassionate outsider. Challenge the assumptions that fortify your beliefs, recognizing that there exists a myriad of perspectives beyond your own.

When seeking guidance, resist the allure of confiding solely in friends and family. Instead, consider the impartiality of a counselor–an unbiased arbiter endowed with the expertise to navigate the complexities of human connections. They bring a fresh, neutral lens to your situation, providing insights that may elude those close to you.

However, be prepared for a journey of self-discovery and honesty upon entering counseling. Embrace the discomfort of confronting truths, perhaps even harsh ones, that compel you to view your relationship from a different angle. It is through this uncomfortable exploration that growth and understanding gracefully emerge.

As we bring this enlightening journey to a close, let us cherish the profound beauty inherent in relationships. They are intricate tapestries woven with shared moments, challenges, and love. Embrace the uniqueness of your connection, savor the joys, and courageously weather the storms together.

In the grand tapestry of life, relationships stand out as the most intricate and captivating threads. So, my esteemed readers, carry the wisdom garnered from this exploration, relish the complexities, and above all, revel in the inherent beauty that relationships paint across the canvas of your life.